INNOVATIONS IN ADMINISTRATION

INNOVATIONS IN ADMINISTRATION

Bharat Lal Meena, IAS

Editor

Pramod Kumar

PRABHAT PRAKASHAN

Published by
PRABHAT PRAKASHAN PVT. LTD.
4/19 Asaf Ali Road,
New Delhi-110 002 (INDIA)
e-mail: prabhatbooks@gmail.com

ISBN 978-93-86300-54-6
INNOVATIONS IN ADMINISTRATION
by Dr. Meenu Sodhi Sharma

Edition
2025

Price
₹ 500.00 (Rupees Five Hundred only)

Printed at
Print Media, New Delhi

Dedicated to my parents,
Father the Late Shri Sukhji Ram and
Mother Smt. Ratani Bai,
for raising me to believe that everything is possible. I am what I am because of them. I am eternally grateful to them for discharging their duties as responsible parents. They are source of inspiration for many others.

Foreword

When the manuscript of this book *'Innovations in Administration'* was given to me by Mr. Bharat Lal Meena, with a request to go through the same and then to see whether I can write the Foreword, my immediate reaction was one of self-doubt about my ability to do justice to such an assignment. Here was an account of the 'life in action' of a refined IAS officer with impeccable credentials, who has gone through full term of thirty years of Government service with highest dedication and professionalism.

As I quickly went through the contents of the manuscript, it became clear to me that Mr. Meena had an extraordinary journey, shouldering responsibilities of varying demands, challenges, and complexities and all this of extremely sensitive nature. It is clear to me that the Officer had to deal with real life problems on the ground, provide pragmatic solutions, oversee the most difficult task of implementation, and above all has ultimate satisfaction in the end because there was no adverse reaction at any stage. One can see this trend persisting all through his service life, day-in and day-out. In fact, this is the typical career life of an IAS officer, requiring speed, efficiency and ensuring pragmatic solutions.

The only rationale, I can see for me being entrusted with this task could be that as a Scientist I too had an unusual journey of shouldering a variety of responsibilities. Beginning my career as a scientist, technologist, and a technocrat, heading a major organisation (Space) and subsequently making forays into the Rajya Sabha, Planning Commission of India, again directing a think-tank, National Institute of Advanced Studies (NIAS), in Bengaluru, and ultimately donning the roles of the Chairman of Karnataka Knowledge Commission and Chancellor of Jawaharlal Nehru University (JNU), New Delhi. These diverse responsibilities were full of unusual challenges. Probably, Mr. Meena thought that if somebody has to have an appreciation of the type of experience that he himself had in his eventful career it could be the people like us.

Nevertheless, I developed lot of appreciation for the IAS cadre during my tenure in ISRO. I closely observed my erstwhile Chairman of ISRO, Prof. Satish Dhawan, as to how he handled the bureaucracy. He had known very closely the brilliant bureaucrats like Mr. M.A. Vellodi, Mr. T.N. Seshan and later Mr. Warrier as Additional and Joint Secretary. Besides interfacing with the complex issues at Delhi level, they fully understood the subtle nuances of managing a complex Space programme. They advised Prof. Dhawan in the most constructive manner even beyond finance and administrative aspects, by anticipating all problems and helping in their solution in the most pragmatic way.

During my own term as Indian Space Research Organisation (ISRO) Chairman for more than nine years, there were some extraordinary bureaucrats, who supported the Department and clearly displayed that their cadre too can provide complimentary and supplementary inputs to the role of the technocrats in providing a total efficient and effective management to the organisation. I especially recall such extraordinary names as Mr. Prabhakaran, Mr. Sisir Das, Mr. Abhijeet Sengupta, Mr. Meenakshi Sundaram, Mr. Ranganath, Mr. P.P. Prabhu, Mr. Nadadoor and many others. I may also mention that most of them were from the Karnataka cadre. Some time they would jokingly remark that they would like to have separate cadres of IAS officers where the brightest of them will get a chance to serve the Department of Space.

Mr. Bharat Lal Meena, by recalling his multiplicity of roles over many years, has created a very interesting and absorbing narrative through 58 chapters, covering nearly 296 pages. His roles obviously take us to several dimensions of the national administrative endeavour overseen and implemented by the bureaucracy of the country. He himself started his civil service career as an officer of the Rajasthan Administrative Service (RAS), graduating subsequently to the Indian Administrative Service (IAS) and later joining the Karnataka cadre. There is a long and varied account of his subsequent responsibilities from being a Block Development Officer in Rajasthan to moving to higher and higher levels, finally becoming the Additional Chief Secretary in the Government of Karnataka, in-charge of Higher Education. In addition to his postings as District Collector, he looked after the Departments of Tourism, Woman and Child Welfare, Mass Education, etc. He also had a short stint at Delhi Central Secretariat in the Ministry of Steel. Getting back to Karnataka his roles included heading the Housing Board, BECSOM, Irrigation, Social Welfare, BBMP, BDA, Agriculture, Urban Development and now the Higher Education.

In an extremely simple narrative, Mr. Meena has explained the challenges that he has faced and the unique situations that he had to handle. It is quite clear from his recollections that each of them needed a separate approach and innovative strategy to be crafted virtually on the spot. In this connection, he proudly remarks that he tried to be sensitive to the views and opinions of his political bosses and also his superiors so that his ability to resolve issues is not faced with bottlenecks.

On the whole, this is an account of a bureaucrat who had successfully steered his career, staying relevant to the system, working towards pragmatic approaches in context to the needs of the country and at the same time being able to provide solutions that are convincing and acceptable to the higher levels. This is something that everyone, belonging to this cadre and allied responsibilities, have to recognise for being successful.

I myself came into contact with Mr. Bharat Lal Meena as Chairman of Karnataka Knowledge Commission (KKC). The Commission was reconstituted by the incumbent Government when Mr. Deshpande was the Minister of Higher Education. When Mr. Meena took over as Principal Secretary, Higher Education, he automatically assumed the administrative responsibilities of the KKC. The KKC is a body of experts who have varied experience in a variety of issues relating to the development of Karnataka and were capable of coming out with unique and out of the box thinking. Most of the time, the thought process from Members needed reviews with the Secretaries of different Departments to ensure feasibility of implementation of the related recommendations. Sometimes the Secretaries themselves come out with certain issues that needed analysis and assessment at the level of KKC. It is in this context, that I found Mr. Bharat Lal Meena extremely active and at ease with this body of intellectuals in having meaningful dialogue. I remember with tremendous admiration his process of thinking and providing inputs to the Education Policy of Karnataka, which had been finalised by the KKC for submission to the Government. An equally important area where he played a proactive role was related to bringing in digital technology in education. In fact, through his own initiatives, he has already introduced technology in the areas of University administration, conduct of examinations, and carrying out classroom lectures. He succeeded in convincing and orienting the Vice Chancellors to adopt digital technology in various aspects of running the Universities in Karnataka. His efforts and knowledge have made extraordinary contributions to the state of Karnataka making it the leading state in bringing technology to the field of education.

On the whole, here is an extraordinary account of an odyssey of a bureaucrat who has shown the way, how to be effective in discharging the roles and responsibilities while being in this important cadre of India's premier Administrative structure. The presentation is lucid, simple, and most importantly besides being informative to the intellectuals and policy-makers it could also serve as a useful guide for those who want to prepare themselves for a variety of competitive examinations. Along with all his colleagues, friends and well-wishers, I would like to pay my rich tributes to Mr. Bharat Lal Meena for his yeomen services to the country, marked by the highest degree of professionalism and excellence. I use this opportunity to congratulate him for writing such a wonderful account of his experience, and sharing the same with the people at large.

—Dr. K. Kasturirangan

Bengaluru

Former Chairman, ISRO

Preface

This is my second book in the series. The first book, titled *'Life and Peace'*, was written long back in 1998-99 focusing on the things that are useful in driving happiness in an individual's life. The idea of writing this book clicked in my mind because of the innovations that I have endeavoured in administration during the last three decades of my service as a Civil Servant. During all these years, I have closely seen the system from within, and it is quite different from how we perceive it from the outside. Probably, the experience that I have gained may serve to guide the new aspirants of Civil Services. Some of the incidents may give them useful tips. That is why I thought to pen them down.

Reliving the Past Experience

Of late, there is a growing perception that most people do not read books. But, we feel that the sale of books is still huge and people do read entertaining and inspiring books. Reviews of many latest books are available in plenty even in the social media. People do read books, which are of their interest and which are useful to them. Therefore, I thought of sharing my experiences. I know that writing a book is not an easy task. It takes a lot of time especially when one is engaged with important assignments of government. Hence, the only time I could spare for it was early in the mornings. My habit of getting up early proved to be very helpful in this task. I have been keeping notes of the various incidents and events since the early days. Basically, I have only elaborated them in this book now. That is how the different chapters have been written. It took about a year to bring the book in the present form. During these months, I have tried to relive my past experiences. The purpose is to share these experiences with others, but for me it is much more like going back to the old times and recollecting, relating, reiterating and cherishing those incidents. Hence, the book is an experience for me to look within myself.

Training at LBSNAA

The book mainly covers the experiences and the milestones that I have achieved in my career starting with the State Civil Service in Rajasthan to the Indian Administrative Service (IAS). It also indicates towards the factors that influenced me during my preparations of Civil Service, and other experiences that I acquired during the probationary period, both in Rajasthan Administrative Service (RAS) and IAS, and the experiences gained along with the colleagues at Lal Bahadur Shastri National Academy of Administration (LBSNAA) in Mussoorie (now in Uttarakhand) during the course of training. Those experiences are quite enriching. The book also reveals how we, the Civil Servants in All India Services come from different cultural and personal backgrounds and how we are planted in different cultural settings. In my case, I was born and brought up in Rajasthan and worked in few other states and finally landed up in South to which I was not exposed earlier. When I was first posted at Lingasugur Sub Division under Raichur District of Karnataka in August 1987, I could not trace on the map where the place was. It was a different experience altogether to come to this region, learning the native language, and identifying with the people, etc.

Purpose of Writing the Book

Despite some deteriorations and negative feedback at times, the Civil Service in India still retains the high level of esteem in public life. In the countryside, people still consider Civil Servants, especially the Collectors, as *'Mai Baap'*, just like during the British colonial period. The role of Civil Servants might have changed, but the perception of people about the Services remains high. The very fact that a large number of aspirants still try every year for Civil Services indicates that. Therefore, if I share my experiences and thoughts, it would give them the opportunity to relate and utilise these experiences in their context. They may find them useful and may look up to them for guidance. That is the purpose of writing this book. Apart from it, there are lots of people who appear for different competitions. They can also get motivated and make up their mind to join the Civil Services. The book also aims at giving them an insight into the Civil Services.

Enjoying Challenging Assignments

One thing that I wish to mention here about my career in Civil Service is that I have always enjoyed good support from the powers that be. I was mostly given the assignments, which were challenging, and I tried my best to live up to their expectations. Probably, the goodwill generated over the period of time is the asset of a Civil Servant. So, in this book, I have tried to share some of those incidents and events which have been able to bring about that goodwill. It covers wide-ranging events starting from my probationary period, Sub Division period, going to the Electricity Board and the wide range of assignments in which I have served in the field and then finally in the Secretariat. In every field that I have worked, there have been challenges pertaining to the Departments. As a Civil Servant, how we respond to those challenges or how we prepare ourselves to face those challenges is itself a challenge. Though the incidents or experiences of others may not be similar to mine, they can give us guidance. Ultimately, the Civil Servant has to have his own strategy to face those challenges. In that sense, every Civil Servant is required to be dynamic to be able to perform, and that requirement is much more now than ever before.

Blocking the Leakage in System

Nowadays people are much more aware than earlier. The people then could be convinced by the leaders, but today it is not so. Because of the advancements in communication and technology, a Civil Servant now has to be accessible and responsive to their needs. The Civil Servants are exposed so much to the needs and sensitivities of the people that they have no option but to perform. It, of course, puts lot of pressure on the Civil Servants today. But, if we see introspectively, challenges were there in the past too. With the time these things too have changed, but then the Civil Servant has to fulfill the aspirations of the people. Now we can see a continuous rise in the aspirations of the people. Their expectations are becoming higher. Every government of the day promises lots of things to people. They also take up large number of populist schemes, which consume lots of resources. Sometimes some constructive things happen, but there are resource constraints too. Then how to involve people and curb leakages in the system are big challenges. Another challenge is that of manpower. In the government system, unlike the private sector, which works on a hire and fire system, one can neither hire nor fire. You have to make the most of the manpower available to you. How to transform, motivate and convert them into a productive force is always a challenge. Since lots of changes are happening around the globe, people expect those changes here too. However, awareness about the duty is very less, the expectations to fulfill the rights is always there.

Going Beyond the Rule Book

The Administration is not just going by the Rule Book. Rules have to be followed, but people do not expect literal interpretation of rules. Many times, you lose the real spirit of law, if you interpret it literally. I have tried to run the administration more by common sense. If we put ourselves in the position of a common man, who is trapped in a particular situation, we will realise his ordeal. In that case, you will not be wrong if you apply common sense. It is very important for a bureaucrat to keep his/her eyes and ears open. They should get information from all possible sources. Feedback should be received not only from the officials, but also from the public, public representatives and from other stakeholders too. What they say has to be heard. Constant dialogue with people is quintessential.

Taking all Stakeholders on Board

The other important aspect that this book aims to highlight is the presence of mind. When a problem arises, the man on the spot must interact with the surrounding. Many a time, we don't mix up with the people. We must keep an open mind. This book makes an effort to do that. The other thing, which it highlights, is the need for dialogue, discussion, interaction and inclusiveness in mind while taking decisions and being open to suggestions. The dynamism in the society is so much that all stakeholders have to work in harmony with one another. Otherwise, the desired results will not be achieved. We may set a goal, but unless we take all the stakeholders on board, it won't be possible to attain that goal.

The book would be helpful for those people who are trying to prepare for the Civil Services. It is also useful for serving Civil Servants and it may be useful for others also who are interested in knowing the management aspects in government system.

To be a successful bureaucrat, I feel, one has to have the support of others. You can't be successful on your own. You need support. In my case, the huge support has always come from my family, my wife and children.

They have always been quite understanding to my official needs and requirements. They never interfered or demanded on the office timings. They have always been accommodative, even if I reached home late or left early. They always understood that it was necessary for me to be able to effectively perform my duties. Their contribution has been immense in whatever experiments I have made in the Civil Service or whatever I have been able to achieve. Of course, there are also many friends and colleagues, who helped and guided me at different occasions. There are also good friends who have helped in bringing out this book. My gratitude is always there to all including the country's eminent scientist and Chairman of Karnataka Knowledge Commission Dr. K. Kasturirangan for writing Forward, New Delhi based senior journalist, researcher and editor of this book Mr. Pramod Kumar, Bengaluru based senior journalist Mr. Venugopalan.

The book shares highlights only. It is not a complete narrative of all the incidents. It covers only certain incidents and milestones, which can reflect the issues relevant today. I have tried to be simple, pure, and straightforward in my narration. The purpose of my narration is not to influence in general, but to share my thoughts from my perspective. I could not mention many things in the book due to paucity of time and space. I am sure it is not the end. There may be many more books to follow.

—Bharat Lal Meena

Bengaluru

EDITOR'S NOTE

The Catalyst for a Meaningful Change

We have 545 Lok Sabha and 245 Rajya Sabha MPs, over 4000 MLAs in state Assemblies, about 1,000 Members of Legislative Councils (MLCs) in seven states, thousands of local body representatives in urban areas and 29,21,382 elected representatives in Village, Intermediate and District Panchayats, including 12,70,350 elected women representatives (as on February 28, 2015) in Panchayats. It shows the representation of all segments in governance from policy formulation to execution and monitoring. Apart from it, there are over 64 lakh government employees and about 50,000 serving Civil Servants, who are generally believed to be possessing extraordinary talent and out of the box vision. Civil Services are the medium of selecting masterminds for governance, which is evident from the fact that in 2015 over 10,00,000 candidates appeared for IAS exams, out of which 180 were recruited. Undoubtedly, many of the people's representatives from Parliament to local bodies too are visionaries.

However, what pains every sensible person is the fact that despite having such a large pool of talent involved in governance since Independence, why have things not changed on the ground adequately, as envisioned by our freedom fighters, while laying down their lives for the motherland? What the voters are promised during elections is scarcely delivered on the ground. Having lost all hopes, most people have now accepted it as their destiny to live with the hardships, underdevelopment, unrestrained corruption, irresponsive administration, unviable planning and unaccountability on the part of the official machinery. The question, which agitates us constantly, is how long will all this continue? The maximum power that a voter has is to change the representatives through elections every five years. The 'leaders' come and show dreams in every election and then vanish into thin air till the next election. After another five years when they reappear, they approach with new package of dreams. This is what is going on endlessly since Independence. The question is 'how long will this go on like this?

The major damage done to the Indian society during all these years since Independence is the promotion of the mindset of depending upon the government for everything, which is contrary to the traditional Indian psyche, culture and ethos. The borderlines between the community and the government were duly demarcated and everybody respected them. The concepts of 'Panch Parameshwar', 'Gram Swaraj' and Self-Rule have always been there in our traditions. Mahatma Gandhi fostered these ideals in modern times. The state had very limited role in settling disputes, digging wells, maintenance of water bodies, opening and running schools, ensuring cleanliness and hygiene, planting of saplings, making of roads, employment generation, etc. The community performed all these tasks with the active participation and contribution of all sections of the society. Well-to-do people contributed money, while others offered physical labour i.e. '*shramdan*'. Power of the state was confined to providing protection and delivering justice, that too with several limitations. The ruling class observed 'Raj Dharma', which was well-defined and well laid down since time immemorial. Any violation of the 'Raj Dharma' could create serious problems for the ruler and could even endanger his power and positions.

Chanakya's classic work *'Arthashastra'* clearly explains the position of a king as the Servant of the State. "A king has no personal likes; it is the likes of the subject that should be followed by him," he observed. The *'Arthashastra'* also mentions that village has been the basic unit of the administration. More importantly, the decision-making process at various institutional levels including the village was democratic and the bulk of power governing people's affairs remained with people's councils at different levels. Even in the early Vedic period, there were four types of councils, viz. 'Sabha', 'Samiti', 'Vidhata' and 'Gana'. Even during Buddha's period this old decentralised pattern with active participation of the people in decision-making process through dialogue and discussion and voting continued uninterruptedly. But during the Medieval and Mughal periods, the process of self-governance of ancient India withered away under the military despotism of the Sultanate of Delhi and the Mughal Empire. Under the British rule, the administration at local level came under the bureaucratic control. However, the British government was aware of the importance and value of the village system. "India's village communities are little republics, having nearly everything they want within themselves, and almost independent of any foreign relations. They seem to last where nothing else lasts. Dynasty after dynasty tumbles down; revolution succeeds revolution, but the village community remains the same. This union of village communities, each one forming a separate little State in itself, has contributed more than any other thing to the preservation of the people of India," writes Sir Charles Metcalfe, the then acting Governor General of India.

The martyrs as well as the great personalities like Swami Vivekananda, Rabindranath Tagore, Vinoba Bhave, Gandhiji, etc. were strongly against making the society entirely dependent upon the government for everything. In

'Hind Swaraj', Gandhiji visualised a system of governance based upon the traditional wisdom of our ancestors, who managed their lives and affairs by themselves without much interference from outside. He was aware that centralised administration becomes the breeding ground of exploitation and corruption. Besides, it also kills the basic spirit of democracy. He opted for the age-old participatory system of democracy, while the British had replaced it with representative system of democracy. Gandhiji strongly believed that the salvation of India lies in the revival of idyllic nature of the village life and the way of self-management of its day-to-day affairs. But, unfortunately, the successive governments in the country did not take concrete steps towards the process of decentralisation. They talked about people's involvement in governance, but did nothing to ensure it in practice. As a result, the dependence on administration continued to increase day by day, and year after year. The high-level corruption, insensitivity, carelessness, unaccountability, nepotism or other ills that we see today in the administration are the outcome of the same erroneous approach adopted by our power-hungry politicians.

It is not that the successive governments have done nothing to ensure welfare of the deprived classes. In fact, much has been done and huge amount of money is still earmarked for this purpose through various schemes. But the fruits of those schemes did not reach the targeted people. Deeply moved by the pathetic situation, the then Prime Minister Rajiv Gandhi in 1988, as a remedy to curb corruption and ensure fruits of power to the needy people, initiated some steps to strengthen public participation in governance by empowering the local self-governance bodies or the Panchayats. His efforts were properly materialised in 1993 when the Narasimha Rao government introduced 73rd and 74th Amendments in the Indian Constitution. But this exercise too proved to be a new medium of siphoning of public funds – only due to lack of genuine public participation. Rajiv Gandhi had in 1988 said that 'for every rupee sent to the common man, only 17 paise reached him'. Instead of improvement, the situation worsened in all these years, as admitted by the then Deputy Chairman of Planning Commission Montek Singh Ahluwalia, who on October 14, 2009 citing a Plan Panel study on PDS, claimed that "only 16 paise out of a rupee reach the targeted poor".

All this shows the lack of honest efforts on the ground to curb corruption or involve people in governance. Apart from the government agencies, we have about 32 lakh registered Non Governmental Organisations (NGOs), as claimed by the Central Bureau of Investigation (CBI) in its affidavit filed in the Supreme Court of India on August 1, 2015. This figure is more than double the number of schools in the country, 250 times the number of government hospitals, one NGO for 400 people as against one policeman for 709 people. Despite the huge number of NGOs the situation on the ground is still disappointing. Most of them seem to be interested in receiving funds from internal or external agencies. The prime question is – how to take the fruits of development to the last person of the society, ensuring health, education, housing, etc. to him.

Under the given conditions, Mr. Bharat Lal Meena, the Karnataka cadre IAS of 1985 batch, emanates a ray of hope. His three decades' long tenure as Civil Servant and the experiments made therein, and his out of the box thinking present an alternative. Right from his first posting as Assistant Commissioner at Lingasugur Sub Division in Raichur District of Karnataka, where he motivated local people to resolve their decades-long drinking water problem permanently, to all other postings in different Departments of the State Government, he left an indelible mark through his out of the box and pragmatic decisions. The key that he adopted for making this change was transformation of the 'I' feeling into the 'We' feeling—the toughest task advocated by all, but achieved by a very few. People admire him mainly for two reasons – one, his focus on permanent solution to the problems and two, ensuring genuine community participation in planning and execution of the government schemes, something that is urgently needed for success of democracy. Mr. Meena is a Civil Servant who never fixed any 'official meeting time' for the general public during his entire tenure and met people whenever they visited him. Many of the 'innovative' schemes like Soil Health Card, Direct Benefit Transfer, Social Audit, Biometric Attendance, computerisation in electricity department, energy audit, opening 24/7 bill payment kiosks in electricity department, etc., which are now being implemented by many states and Central Government, were tried, tested and successfully implemented by Mr. Meena in Karnataka long back. However, the mainstream media failed to notice those innovative steps.

It is noteworthy that the Government of India implemented Direct Benefit Transfer (DBT) scheme to distribute and disburse the grants directly to beneficiaries under various social welfare schemes since January 1, 2013, and also biometric attendance for all employees since September 2014. But Mr. Meena introduced these practices successfully in Social Welfare Department of Karnataka Government way back in the year 2008. In 1992, as Chief Secretary of Zilla Parishad, Shimoga, he changed the way the schemes should be planned and implemented on the ground level, thus receiving laurels from all quarters. He ensured the successful implementation of social audit scheme as well.

The impact of his initiatives is visible in thousands of villages of Karnataka in the form of self-reliance activities, 100 per cent literacy, waste management and technological advancement. He has succeeded in developing debt-free, smoke-free, plastic-free and hut-free and no dues villages, an extraordinary feat for an IAS official, as most of them want to play as masters and not as civil 'servants'. As a restless crusader, he has inspired thousands of youngsters, women and people of all age groups, both in rural and urban areas, to toil for the underprivileged and bring a change in their lives. There are innumerable examples, where the local people, inspired by him actively joined hands with the administration for resolving their problems themselves – literally ousting the nexus of contractors and corrupt officials. Whether it was for restoration of the old tanks, construction of bus shelters, building or repairing of school or Anganwadi buildings, roads, playgrounds, planting saplings, developing parks, maintaining hygiene, conducting health camps, blood donation camps, campaigning against liquor, plastic, dowry or other social evils, promoting self-reliance or even conducting literacy classes, all could be done with active participation and involvement of the local people. Whitewashing of 1,200 public buildings by the people in one day on January 26, 1993 in Shimoga District of Karnataka was not an ordinary feat. It not only put an effective check on corruption, but also ascertained the association of local people with the project from the core of their hearts.

At the time when most NGOs are seen busy in money-making business, Mr. Meena sets a precedent of social service too. He formed 'Apnadesh Association' as a voluntary organisation in 1991, which neither collects donations nor provides monetary help to anyone. 'Apnadesh' mostly takes up the activities, which do not require money at all. That is why during all these years the 'Apnadesh' transformed the people's mindset to the extent that they take different pledges like making their village plastic-free, dispute-free, 100 per cent literate, etc, and strive to achieve those targets collectively. 'Apnadesh' has prepared a list of over 100 activities, which can be carried out without funds. What is required is only the change in mindset. These experiments are eye-opener for other policymakers. The question is, if one Meena can do so many wonders, why not the other bureaucrats, MPs, MLAs, Panchayat or Municipality members?

Mr. Bharat Lal Meena seems to be a master of development studies, and no doubt, he is endowed with the unique gift of spiritual wisdom, creative thinking, positive outlook, humanitarian approach, spirit of voluntarism and on top of all the skills of management, including life management, without which qualities it is just not possible for any of us to serve the people – to think freely, to design, and to implement useful policies in the interest of the common man selflessly. I don't know whether anyone would ever heed to my suggestion, but I still want to make it that Mr. Meena would prove to be the best available resource person for running 'Orientation Programmes' for the Civil Servants who have completed at least 5-10 years of service.

However, this book endeavours to bring forth some of the creative steps taken by Mr. Bharat Lal Meena. It has deliberately been divided into small chapters so that readers understand the issues properly. In the beginning of some of the chapters, a core issue has been highlighted in box so that the readers understand the impact of Mr. Meena's initiatives in proper perspective. The book may prove to be highly useful for serving bureaucrats, management professionals, students, policymakers, researchers, people's representatives and also for those who are preparing for Civil Service exams. This also acquaints the readers with some of the undisclosed facts about Mr. Meena's personal life – how he decided to quit the IAS immediately after joining it, his quest for spirituality, three jobs before joining the IAS, and so on.

My task remains incomplete without extending my sincere thanks to eminent scientist and former Chairman of the Indian Space Research Organisation (ISRO) Dr. K. Kasturirangan for writing Forward of the book. I also express my thanks to Shri Venugopalan, senior journalist and Group Editor of *'Apnadesh Samachar'* and Dr. Shakti Kumar Pandey, Professor of English, for helping me in gathering information and presenting the book in present form.

—Pramod Kumar

New Delhi

Contents

Acquainting with the Basics of Administration

Two years stint as a Rajasthan Administrative Service Probationer and Block Development Officer in Anta under Kota District of Rajasthan during 1983-85

I joined the Rajasthan Administrative Service (RAS) in 1983 and was there till 1985. As happens with other services also, we were initially sent for a training programme at Officers Training School (now known as Harish Chandra Mathur Rajasthan State Institute of Public Administration) in Jaipur. It is one of the best training institutes for officers in the country. There was a Director there, Mr. Meethalal Mehta, a very down to earth bureaucrat who was very well known for his integrity and numerous other qualities. He used to deliver motivational talks and apprise us of the practical aspects. I still remember some of the lessons I learned from him. He used to say that our roots must be grounded like the bamboo and we should not be above the ground. Another thing he stressed upon was flexibility so that we can move in any direction without being rigid. He also shared his administrative experience of facing the drought and other such situations. It was all very inspiring.

Imbibing Out of the Box Vision

Before 1983 there was a devastating flood. A part of that

Institute was washed away by a nullah. Then, Mr. Mehta came up with the idea of planting lots of trees as Smriti Van. Those who visited there planted trees in the memory of their near and dear ones. Subsequently, the place became very popular. Lots of trees were planted there, thus creating a lot of greenery.

We found the training very interesting. Ours was one of the biggest batches. During the training a lot of learning took place amongst the probationers. An incident took place in 1984 when the then Prime Minister Smt. Indira Gandhi was assassinated. As the news spread, there was violence everywhere. One of the probationers was from the Sikh community. Since there was news of harassing and killing the Sikhs, we advised him not to venture out and stay inside the room only. We could see how the fear had percolated in the minds of the people then.

Then we were posted in Kota District for further training. An IAS probationer was also there at that point of time. We used to discuss many things with him. I realised that on many subjects he had theoretical knowledge, but I thought practically. Even then, he had his own ideas. We saw different people came on different administrative posts. They have their own particular thought process.

Two Faces of Same Person

In Collector's Office, we saw people coming in delegations. When the leaders of those delegations were in the public, they used different language, calling the Officers as white elephants who do nothing. But as they would enter the Collector's Chamber, their language used to be quite different. They spoke very politely, and with high regard. When we simply asked them about the drastic change in their language, tone and tenor from what they were saying outside to how they were behaving inside, they said if they said all good things in public, who would come to them. We know well what can be done by the Administration and what not. I saw the same persons talking two languages. That is learning, and that is what happens at most places.

Studying the Damage Caused in Communal Riots

One day we got the message that we have to rush to a tehsil headquarters Mangrol, where communal riots had broken out and lots of shops were being selectively burnt. We went there by jeep. We went to the Police Station, where huge damage was caused by the rioters. We also visited the affected areas and damage assessment was done. We were only probationers; others were doing the actual work. We also went there with the DIG of Police for early morning inspections. When we were passing through an inside area, we heard a person and inquired about him. A person was lying in a nullah, neck half chopped and his throat was slit with a sharp weapon. He was unable to lift his head. He was crying in pain. He said he was a Hindu and other community people were chasing him. He was quickly lifted and admitted to a hospital in Kota for treatment. Then the Magistrate was called to record his dying declaration. In the dying declaration that person revealed his real name. He was a Muslim, but feared that some Hindus were chasing him. He thought if he revealed his real Muslim name, they'd kill him. Finally, he survived miraculously. Later, many peace committee meetings were convened and normalcy was restored. There are lots of such experiences.

Resolving the Problems of Villagers

Then on, I was posted as a Block Development Officer (BDO) in Anta, which was then part of Kota District. Since I was alone there, I interacted with all the Gram Panchayat Members and Sarpanchs establishing direct rapport with them and understanding their problems. Anta was comparatively a fertile area, but there were lot of fund constraints—half work done, that too with poor quality. But, finally we could resolve those problems by planning and releasing the funds. Field inspection helped in a big way at the time.

Rajasthan Administrative experience was like a basic foundation for me. We were able to prevent violence and other such incidents in Karnataka several times because of the experience I gained from this stint. It helped me a lot. Experience is always valuable.

□

Learning the Art of Scaling High

Training at Lal Bahadur Shastri National Academy of Administration (LBSNAA), Mussoorie, in 1985

Training period is indeed an unforgettable phase in the career of an Officer. That is a time when they don't have any responsibility and get the opportunity to meet so many people. During the course of training, they are told about their future responsibilities and the powers that will be vested in them. Some very interesting incidents happen during that period.

At the Lal Bahadur Shastri National Academy of Administration (LBSNAA), Mussoorie (now in Uttarakhand), where our Foundation Course was going on, there were over 1,000 Officers of all the Services put together. That is the time you meet people of all Services together at one place. Subsequently, you also develop friendship with the people who are not in the IAS. You may get the opportunity to meet your IAS friends many times during the Service period, but those who are outside IAS rarely meet in the later stages of their careers.

Cross Country Runner

Training is a time when you mix up with so many people from across the country. It is very interesting, as it gives you lots of memories to cherish throughout the life. During the Foundation Course, a Cross-Country Run used to be organised once in a month. It used to be announced one day before only. Some people prepared for it, as it was a 13 km run around the hills of Mussoorie. Lots of ups and downs were there en route. It was quite exhausting. I never had thought of participating in the Run. I enjoyed spending time with the probationers and also playing cards. Sometimes we used to play whole night.

In the morning when the Run was to begin, I got up hurriedly, freshened up and started running. Because, I was from a rural background and maintained healthy food habits, I kept on running and running. Some people were left behind, while some were exhausted. Finally, upon the completion of the Run, I came first. Second was a faculty member, Mr. Julius. Second time also, I kept running and stood first. Similarly, third time too, I stood first. So, I was the Cross-Country Runner in all the three races during my time in the Academy.

Another interesting thing that happened then was the Pairings. The unmarried officers started looking for a partner. Every day, we used to hear gossip of somebody going with X and someone with Y. My roommate, who got into Police service subsequently, used to pass comments on a girl sitting next to him. After sometime, she invited him to help her to study. He went there twice. Then he started describing her body in a derogatory manner. But after some time, he got into the serious relationship with the same girl. Finally, he ended up marrying her. This is how serious relationships develop.

Bharat Darshan

Another interesting thing during training period was

Bharat Darshan. During the Tour, all the trainees were taken to different places of the country. We went to North-East. I preferred North-East because most people normally do not go there. I had been there long back after completing MA. So, I wanted to explore North-East a little more.

When we went there, some people had the habit of occupying the better rooms in the guest houses when the bus reached the destination. They did not even leave the good rooms for ladies or officers. They occupied them quickly. Some people also had the habit of not even picking up their own luggage. Nobody was there to pick up the luggage. We were a few of us, who took everyone's luggage down and then reached the guest house. We did that kind of work also during the Bharat Darshan tour.

Like Attracts Like

There is another bad habit in some people. During the journey, some people start fighting on which song should be played and which not. Everyone has different tastes. Somebody says he/she does not like Hindi songs, while some said they do not like songs from other languages. The people with such mean mentality were also there. They fought like as if they were fighting in the street. We were taken to Bharat Darshan basically to know the nature of the people.

True learning happens when you are together with someone. Then only you come to know the real nature of a person. On the face, we talk goody-goody for few minutes and have good impression of the person. But when you stay together with someone or travel with them only then you know the real nature of that person. The purpose of taking us on the Tour was also to help us develop a good bond. You like some people life-long and that friendship stays together for years. Those who are short tempered or indulge in backbiting are disliked by most. Once you know their real nature, you start keeping them apart. Like attracts like. Such people like only such people. We used to have interesting things like this.

Decision to Quit IAS

Indian Administrative Service (IAS) was my fourth job. I had a very strange notion of proving that I have achieved something. So, I wanted to quit the Service after joining it. I thought I should announce that I have left the Service after passing it. That idea used to crop up in my mind very frequently. But then I calmly thought over what I would do if I quit the Service. After all, one has to work somewhere. Without work one cannot live. Then I realised that it would be foolish to leave the Service and do any other work. If you are not successful in your career, you condemn yourself for the rest of your life. Then I felt it would be a wrong decision to leave the Service.

Opportunity to Introduce Desired Changes

Another thing is that you can bring about a better change while staying inside the system. Being in the system, you can fight with the system better. If you fight from outside, the whole system is against you. If you are part of the system, you can bring the desired changes at least within your areas of responsibility.

Then, finally, good sense prevailed in me and I decided to continue in the Service. That is the sense that drives me in all my assignments that I took up during all these years in the Service.

In every assignment, I tried to do something out of the box, something different, and something that I think is a value addition to the system from my side. That paid dividends to me. That is the good thing that I have learnt during my service period. Now, I don't regret my decision of staying inside the system. Go in the direction your heart tells you. The heart never betrays you.

□

SCARCITY OF WATER

Water is life, but it is also the most neglected and misused natural resource today. No doubt, scarcity of drinking water, due to the growing human population, severe neglect and over-exploitation, is a global concern India is most vulnerable because of the growing demand and undisciplined lifestyle. According to Government statistics, the per capita water availability in India in 1951 was about 5177 cubic meters, which reduced to about 1545 cubic meters in 2011 and it is expected to reduce to 1341 cubic meters by the year 2025 and 1140 cubic meters by 2050.

Surely, India is blessed with a good rainfall—an average of 1170 mm annually. The total available sweet water in the country is 4000 billion cubic meters per annum. Out of it, over 1047 billion cubic meters is lost due to evaporation, transpiration and runoff. Only 18% of the rainwater is used effectively, while 48% enters the rivers, most of which reaches the ocean. Out of the total usable water, 728 billion cubic meters is contributed from surface water and 395 billion cubic meters is contributed by replenishable ground water. Pollution of water bodies is another major concern. Although, 5% of the total water is used for domestic use, 27% of the villages and 4 to 6% urban population in the country do not have access to potable water. Over 70% of the water consumed by rural population in India does not meet the WHO standards. Despite all these concerns, India is bound to face severe scarcity of water in the future. Therefore, it is necessary to prevent it by making the best use of the available technologies and resources to conserve the existing water resources. Reviving the traditional water bodies, the prime source of water in our country since centuries, is need of the hour.

Fruits of Collective Efforts

First posting as Assistant Commissioner from August 1987 to August 1989 at Lingasugur Sub Division of Raichur District

"Sincerity of conviction and purity of motive will surely gain the day; and even a small minority, armed with these, is surely destined to prevail against all odds." These priceless words of Swami Vivekananda have been a guiding force for me. It is my firm belief that if you do any work with full conviction, people support you and despite all odds, you are able to achieve the desired results. This is the reason I could dare take so many out of the box initiatives in the Administration and took them to their logical conclusion. I realised the fruits of collective efforts during my first posting at Sindhanur Taluk under Raichur District in 1987, where we resolved the decade's long drinking water problem with the active participation of the local people. In fact, the experiment kick-started a movement in the state where public and officials joined hands to resolve problems.

Sindhanur is a Taluk and Block Headquarters in Raichur District. It is located on Bidar-Srirangapatnam National Highway linking North to South of Karnataka. The area is very fertile and well irrigated. It is an Urban Town. The richness and affluence had hidden an acute problem faced by the local population. It had a severe drinking water shortage until 1988 when we resolved it. Daily supply of pure drinking water was a pipe dream of people until 1988. Untreated water used to be supplied to some parts of the town and that too once a week or sometime in 10 days. Many families were unable to get brides, as outsiders (parents of the girls) never wanted to marry their daughters in this town mainly because of the acute problem of drinking water.

Changing the Mindset of Official Machinery

For tackling this problem, the then Deputy Commissioner of Raichur District sanctioned a sum of Rs. two lakh to tide over the problem during summers. As Assistant Commissioner, I visited the spot where the water used to be stored. A temporary earthen bund used to be constructed every year across a nullah to store the water. Since the area was not protected and fenced, animals also used to drink water there. Some people used it to bathe and wash dirty linen too. That untreated water used to be pumped directly for drinking to the people. Seeing that state of affairs, I decided not to give any money for the temporary work, which used to be done during every rainy season. Instructions were given to create a permanent storage area where investment once made would not go waste. Karnataka Urban Water Supply and Drainage Board Engineers were uncooperative and said no other alternative existed.

Local People Join Hands

I instructed the Revenue Officials to scout for Government land. Promptly they came with details of Government land measuring over 15 acres behind the Government College in Sindhanur on Kustagi Road. It was an abandoned PWD quarry. Having got the land, the next challenge was to execute the work within the limited resources (₹ 2 Lakh only) and without technical support. I had heard that heavy machinery, which was used to build Narayanpur Dam across Krishna River, was parked idle in the Irrigation Department Camp. I enquired about the condition of those equipments – scrappers, dozers, etc. The drivers told that most of the equipments were in good condition. I borrowed them from the Irrigation Department and pressed them into service with only the POL expenses incurred from our side.

The work started in full swing immediately. No proper engineering plan existed. The idea was to dig a reservoir to impound water. Lots of prominent citizens came to the spot and enquired from me as to what the plan was. I told them that I am creating an impounding reservoir and will continue work till the time the amount of ₹ 2 lakh lasts. I asked them if they wanted the work to continue. All of them said yes, and then I suggested them to constitute a Citizens Committee (Nagrik Samiti) and raise resources from public for the project.

Government Gave ₹ 2 Lakh, Public 25 Lakh

To my utter surprise, I found that cutting across all party lines, they constituted a Nagrik Samiti and within few days, they raised over ₹ 25 lakh. I advised them against depositing the money with the Government. The Committee took over the responsibility of supervising the construction work. The work continued. It was a period when President's Rule was in force. The prominent leaders came together and took it up with the Governor and got a regular scheme sanctioned with Tungabhadra River as the source, which was just over 30 km from there. After few years, the regular scheme was completed. They made another proper reservoir. The old impounding reservoir was preserved separately and is still fondly called 'Meena Kere' (Meena's Tank).

The collective efforts made by Assistant Commissioner, people, and the departments bore fruit and even today every household remembers the difficulties they faced back then and the benefits they enjoy today. This experiment encouraged me to form a voluntary organisation to mobilise public support and motivate them to actively join hands in government projects. Finally, the experience of working with people in the field, coordinating with various departments was highly rewarding and enriching.

The Greatest Gain of My Life

We could do that because our intentions were clear and objective was pious. Public interest was the only agenda and the work from beginning to end was done with full transparency. When you do anything honestly and people realise your bona fide intentions, they come forward to help you. At many occasions during my service spanning about three decades I have realised it. People supported us beyond our expectations in many initiatives. This public trust is the greatest capital that I have earned in my service. The Lingasugur experiment shows that individual efforts can bring excellence, but only collective efforts can deliver effectively.

□

Acquiring Negotiation Skills

Computerised Karnataka Electricity Board (KEB) as Secretary from October 17, 1989 to August 1, 1991

From Lingasugur I went to Health and Family Welfare Department as Deputy Secretary for a brief period from August 4, 1989 to October 16, 1989. Then I was posted as Secretary, Karnataka Electricity Board (KEB), on October 17, 1989. The KEB at that point of time was a single entity covering both transmission and distribution activities. The generation activity was separated in 1971 by creating the KPCL. The KEB was a monolithic organisation covering the entire state. Therefore, there were issues always pertaining to power supply, grievances of the people, wrong billing, etc. So, there were departmental enquiry cases also.

There were mainly two wings in the KEB—Technical and Administration. The Technical wing was handled by an Additional Secretary, while I oversaw the Administration part. I was Secretary to Electricity Board also. The KEB then did not have a Member Secretary. In some states, however, the post of Secretary was also Member Secretary, who took part in the proceedings of the Board and give opinion on various issues. But, in KEB, the views of the Secretary were not taken into account. That way there were some limitations.

Concentration on Administrative Reforms

As I started the work and started discussing issues with

the people, I became aware of many intricacies. My major concerns were introducing reforms, fast disposal of the files and looking after the administrative issues. I focused more on the disposals of the pending papers fast, making the local officers dispose the administrative matters fast, etc. During this tenure, I had to undertake negotiations with the employees' unions. Since the wage revisions used to take place every four years, the Unions would give a charter of demands to the management, which negotiated with them and arrived at some consensus. That was what I did back then.

Computerisation in the Board

I found the employees' unions were very strong in KEB. They were indeed thoroughly professional in their job. They knew everything. There was one general secretary, Mr. Pandit, who knew much more than even an officer as far as the employees' issues were concerned. He could recite the KEB orders, references, what happened at which time, etc. from his memory. They were very good at negotiating. Naturally, we had to develop better negotiating skills, which I learnt from them. We had a Chairman, though for a limited period, who had a vision in mind. We had discussions with him on how to introduce good initiatives in the Board.

As part of the reforms, a major initiative was introduction of computers in the Board. In those days, computers were a rarity. The economy was opening-up and economic reforms had just begun at the central level. At that time, the Chairman even suggested to take the Union leaders en block and expose them to some countries where reforms or computerisation had taken place, so that they become aware of it and do not oppose the reforms process. We planned it, but it could not materialise due to some reasons. On the administrative front, I tried to do a lot of what was within my capacity.

Quick Disposal of Departmental Enquiries

I disposed of most of the departmental enquires in a very short period. There were about 400 such enquiries at the time and I reduced them to a few—even less than 50. I used to decide the cases in one or two hearings. People had many other problems too such as pension, wages, etc. We did that too. Lots of reforms including sitting arrangements, disposal of files, etc. were introduced. We planned for long term basis. However, we could not succeed much at that moment but that laid the foundation for the reforms. The reasons included pressure from the employees' unions, frequent changes of Chairmen, etc. Those reform plans were way ahead of their time. We could not implement many of them, but the KEB experience helped me at later stages when I was posted in BESCOM and KPTCL. I could start from the day one there because I knew the background, need to make changes, need of public service, etc. One thing was sure that the service provided to the customers was unsatisfactory. That, we could always feel. One of the prime reasons for that was that it was a big organisation.

Opposition from Employees Unions

The employees were hesitant to accept the changes. They felt their numbers would be reduced, they may be retrenched or new recruitment would not take place. They never thought that it would improve their efficiency. Over minor matters they would threaten to go on strike. The employees always had some or the other issue with the government. But they were heard, because it concerned every person in the state. The government always listened to them. That was the kind of value they enjoyed at that time. However, sometimes they used to be very rude to the Officers. Typically, all the unions used to be like that in those days. Subsequently, things have changed now. But, in KEB days it was different. It was a good learning experience for me. I could see how the entire mechanism works, as it was like a public-sector undertaking, a company and like a Board.

It all shows that we should remain a student for lifetime. You should be ready and yearn to learn from every moment of life.

□

A Voyage to Find Oneself
Fascinating Experience of the Kailash Mansarovar Yatra

In 1989, I was posted to the Karnataka Electricity Board (KEB) as Secretary and was in-charge of the Administrative matters. I endeavoured to introduce several reforms in the administrative system. It was all going well. Suddenly, an interesting thing happened. I saw an advertisement in a newspaper about the Kailash Mansarovar Yatra, conducted by the Ministry of External Affairs annually. On enquiry, I found that if somebody joins the Yatra as a Leader of the Group, all expenses are borne by the Ministry of External Affairs. Normally, the officers from Indian Foreign Service (IFS) get this opportunity, and the chances for others in that capacity are minimal. However, I never tried for that, some intuition developed in my mind that I too should take part in the Yatra.

Permission to Join as Sportsperson

Since I was posted in the KEB, I sought permission from the Chairman, who denied the permission saying that was a religious thing, and without government permission they could not allow. I wrote to the DPR explaining that I want to join the Yatra not as a pilgrim, but as a sportsperson because of my trekking hobby. The Chairman thought that the permission would not come, but I got the permission.

Finally, I got the opportunity to join the Kailash Mansarovar Yatra. I did not know much about the significance of the Yatra till then. I had just heard about it. Also, I had not met anyone who had already been there.

Amazing Experience of Trekking

It was about 8 to 10 days of bus journey and then 22 days of trekking in the Himalayas beginning from Pithoragarh, now in Uttarakhand. Every day, we trekked for 10 to 15 km. The path was very interesting. It was amazing to pass through the Himalayan ranges. Various base camps were there and we met many army personnel on our way. When we went to any army camp, lots of people searched for people from their hometowns or nearby areas. So, many people from Rajasthan met us and we had very good cultural programmes. They treated us as their family guests. There were about 30-32 people in a group and total seven groups were allowed that year. It was so homely to meet those army-men at those high altitudes of more than 10,000 feet above the sea level. We were trekking on the Indian side, but the actual Mansarovar lies in the Tibet autonomous region of China.

Wonderful Site of 'Om Parvat'

The people, who do not get a visa, go to the smaller mountain called 'Chhota Kailash', which is on the Indian side. It is a smaller peak where people go, trek and return. On the way, we also came across several mountains in the Himalayan range. There is a place called 'Om Parvat', on reaching which you can see the 'Om' formation on the opposite mountain, which lies across the River. Normally, it is cloudy there, but when the sky is clear, the rock formation is such that there is snow in that area and from a distance it appears like 'Om' is written on the mountain. It was a wonderful sight.

Broad Image of Lord Shiva on the Mountain

When we reach the end of the Indian side and Chinese territory begins, there is a sudden downward slope in that region. There is a lot of snow in that area. So, it is not easy to trek there. People hold each other's hands and go one-by-one stepping very cautiously. Sometimes, you have to carry your luggage too. Porters are there, but you too have to carry some of the luggage. Then we reach a small Chinese town. Only after that we get the bus service—a very ordinary and simple bus, which takes us to Kailash. There is no metaled road there. It is a hilly region without a proper road. After crossing numerous river streams, we reached the base camp in China. When you go closer to the Kailash Mountain, you see other mountains too, which are bare naked sans any snow. It is only on the Kailash Mountain that you see snow. However, the other peaks too have similar elevation, but there is no snow covering them. Even then it is highly fascinating.

It is a place from where you can visualise the image of Lord Shiva—the hair formation, the eyes formation, etc. on the mountain. From a distance, you can clearly make out that it is the statue of Lord Shiva. It was quite amazing. I was surprised to see that such thing can happen. Earlier, we had seen 'Om' mountain, then we saw the image of Lord Shiva. On the way there, on the left side is 'Ravan Taal', where legend goes that Ravana performed his '*tapasya*'. On the right is the Mansarovar Lake. Even if it is snowing and everything freezes, the water in this lake never does. After enjoying that adventure, we went back to the first base camp in China. But what we saw there was very disheartening and disappointing.

Disappointing Scene in Chinese Territory

It was a very small hamlet in China where we halted. But, it was highly disheartening to see the local youngsters preparing and eating non-vegetarian food, openly consuming and selling alcohol and indulging in many other illegal activities too. What pained us was to see that there was no consideration of the sanctity of that pious place. China, which has occupied that place in Tibet, interferes in their cultural aspect too. The younger generation there is almost spoiled in that sense. I don't know what the state policy was, it was not the real Tibet that we see or read outside. Anyway, we spent some time there.

Aspiring to Touch the Mount Kailash

Next day, we had to conduct the *Parikrama* of the Kailash. So, we went to the next base camp, which was behind the Kailash Mountain—about 12 km from the previous base camp. We reached there before lunch and after lunch we did not have any other work. Again, it occurred to me that I must touch Mount Kailash. Something from inside told me that I should touch the holy mountain and bring back pure water from there. I discussed it with a couple of people and asked whether they'd like to accompany me, but they refused. Nevertheless, I took a plastic can and went ahead alone.

After crossing a small River Stream, when I went ahead, I saw the Mountain in front of me. There was no path to go ahead, as if nobody had been there for years. One has to climb every stone and jump to the next. From a distance, you can see the Mountain and if you look to your back you can see the camp. In half an hour's time, I reached the rear side of the Mount Kailash. Suddenly, I saw the Mountain. Normally, the Mountain is slopy, but it was a vertical 90 degree slope. It was like a slip valley, as if the stone had slipped looking like a 90-degree wall. When I looked at that mountain to my surprise I could imagine Lord Shiva from the front side, and at the back, I could visualise the cracks formed in such a manner that the snow formed an image of a lady—as if it was a drawing of goddess Parvati made in nature, carved in the mountain itself. I was surprised to see that—water was melting and snow was on the top. So, I drank lot of water there and came back to the base camp with some water in my can. When, I narrated the whole incident to my fellow travelers, they and the porters said it was very dangerous to go there alone, as wild animals inhabited that area. Lots of snakes were also there. But I returned safely. This was an enthralling adventure I enjoyed that time.

'Parikrama' of Mansarovar Lake

Our group leader, an IFS officer, made me the leader of the group and told me to take care of the day-to-day affairs. The team was good, so I could handle them properly. They were all very happy. Further, we went to the next camp, which was the highest point we climbed. The people who cannot afford to walk hire and ride a Yak. Then we crossed a mountain called Ridge, situated at over 19,000 feet above the sea level. That was the highest point, and many of us started feeling restless due to shortage of oxygen. However, I did not have any problem. Then we climbed down and returned to the base camp. We stayed there for a day and took another round of the *parikrama* of the Mansarovar Lake again. The Bus didn't go to the *parikrama* point and one has to walk and trek in that area. Then we returned to the Chinese town where we had reached upon entering China.

Blissful Experience

The experience of the trekking was so vivid and fulfilling that it is still afresh in my memory, as if it was only yesterday. After returning, I came to know about an Association of the people who have visited the Mansarovar. They keep record of the people who have visited the Kailash. The Association also has a chapter in Bangalore. There are a few people who go there annually. I have met people who have been there seven or eight times. When we came back, they invited us to share our experiences.

Trekking on the Magical Land

You feel something different in that magical region—spirituality, vibration, intuition, etc. The place is completely different. You experience a blissful feeling there. Even if you do not believe in God, you feel something from inside. Such a pious place it is! Now the trekking routes have changed. One can now go there from Himachal Pradesh side also. There is a helicopter service too. Now people can go and return in few days after completing the entire Yatra. But you cannot have the amazing experience that one enjoys in trekking, walking, taking a bus, enjoying the local cuisine, meeting people en route, meeting army men, visiting army camps, etc. For those who haven't yet experienced this Yatra, I would just say, try it – its pure bliss!

□

GENUINE PUBLIC PARTICIPATION

The top-down model of development has failed to ensure equal fruits of governance to all segments of the population. The underprivileged sections such as small and marginal farmers, SCs/STs, women, etc did not fully benefit from the poverty alleviation and development programmes. It is widely realised that there will be no balanced development unless the people are involved in planning and controlling the development process. Local level planning promotes participation of people at grass roots level. Participatory planning involves the people in the process of problem identification, prioritisation and plan preparation. It also promotes a sense of transparency and accountability.

Village Panchayats have been strengthened all over the country by substantially empowering them financially. But this has neither ensured genuine participation of people in planning and execution of the schemes nor could it curb corruption about which former Prime Minister Late Rajiv Gandhi had said during eighties that "for every rupee sent to the common man, only 17 paisa reached him". Instead of any improvement, the situation has only worsened in all these years. It is a major challenge before the planning and execution agencies. The ideal condition will be that the people wholeheartedly connect to the government projects and instead of thinking about stealing anything from the Scheme, they think of contributing on their part whether in the form of cash, kind or time. Those who cannot contribute monetarily can join the projects by performing 'shramdan'. *Karnataka is a model worth emulating in this regard, where this has successfully been done at several places during the last two-three decades.*

Development through Community Participation

Chief Secretary, Zilla Parishad, Belgaum, from August 1991 to January 1992

I was posted in Belgaum as the Administrator of Zilla Parishad in 1991 after completing my tenure in the Karnataka Electricity Board (KEB). The term of the elected body was supposed to end in six months. So, I could work with the elected body only for six months. It was my first interaction with elected representatives. The Chairperson and most of the elected members in the Parishad were very nice and cordial.

Construction of 300 Rooms in Schools through Community Participation

In the beginning, my perception about people's participation was not very positive as I found that the action plan was not as per the requirements on the ground. When I visited the places, I found that people were demanding something else. Many villagers came to me saying that certain work is required to be done. If the work is not a part of the sanctioned plan, it cannot be sanctioned. Therefore, I used to say 'if the work is important, you people collectively contribute something in cash or kind or physical labour'. I had been vested with the power to sanction 5 to 10% discretionary funds. The people agreed to mobilise their contributions. This is how we sanctioned lot of work such as Anganwadi, milk society or school buildings. At that time, we constructed about 300 school rooms in Belgaum alone through this initiative. It became a very interesting experiment. I was also interested in starting such things. I registered 'Apnadesh Association' to galvanise the public support for it. Like minded officials also joined hands with us. We arranged for some office space where we used to sit together after office hours to discuss what can be done further. We also started many other activities like plantation on the roadside.

Desilting the Tank through Shramdan

There is a place Fort Kere in Belgaum from where I used to pass every day. The sewage water was stinking there. There were talks to resolve the problem by converting the place into a commercial site. I did not like the idea as the place was next to the Fort and the Circuit House. I passed a resolution, as the elected body was not there at that time, sanctioning Rs. five lakh for desilting the tank. Though the Tank was in urban area, the command area was rural. The village people got benefited from that. We started desilting the tank and lots of local people joined the work voluntarily. Many people offered *shramdan* (offering to labour voluntarily). We also issued a press note appealing to the public to enroll in for *shramdan*. To our surprise, thousands of people came forward for registration. Then we had to give them time slots. It was basically a rallying point. It connected them to the tank. The army also then offered help. This is how thousands of volunteers under different banners or NGOs joined in to work. It continued as a movement and became a big hit. The then MP and Deputy Commissioner also visited the site. When developed, it became a picnic hot spot. Since, it was very difficult to remove the silt outside the Tank, we created an island inside the Tank itself. The sewage water, which used to fall in the tank, was temporarily diverted.

Then the untreated water was not allowed to enter the Tank. Rain water was allowed though.

The Chief Minister's Commendation

Later, after my transfer the next Deputy Commissioner also continued the work. The people built roads, developed a park and installed benches, etc. around the Tank. Even today that tank remains to be a major tourist attraction. During the Assembly Session, the then Chief Minister also commented how nicely the Tank was restored. However, they did not know about the background of the restoration work. The people enjoyed the work. Even today, if you visit there, people feel happy. Thousands of people enjoy that surrounding. It also expressed the environmental concern associated with that work.

Similar Experiments in Other Towns

There are many other examples where we engaged local people in similar works. In Hukkeri town also, a scheme was sanctioned. A tank was there, but rising line was not there. When I asked the engineers what the problem was, they said labour was unavailable. Then too we adopted the same formula, which we had tried successfully in Belgaum. We asked the local NGOs and associations for support and they agreed. We divided the nine km stretch into meters—which was divided into stretches on a few hundred meters and allocated to NGOs and such organisations which had come forward to help depending upon their capacity. The entire stretch was earmarked. We could lay the rising line of the nine km with the support of people. In Bhoj and other towns also, similar experiments were conducted. Several hundred new buildings were constructed. School betterment committees were activated and local support was mobilised. Lot of tree plantation was also done. Those trees provided new avenues for the local people.

Eleven Wonderful Months

Apart from the developmental work, the involvement of people became so intimate in Belgaum that 'Apnadesh' gained a good foundation. It was no more a paper organisation, it worked on the ground. We also found good media support. Belgaum has a good tradition of cooperation. People are hard-working and the staff is very professional. You need not instruct them to work a hundred times. It was a wonderful experience to work there. I was there only for 11 months, but what we did in those 11 months was like 11 years. The day my transfer orders appeared in newspapers, the then Chief Minister Mr. S. Bangarappa was to visit there. When he was in the Circuit House, some MLAs asked him how come he transferred such a good officer. The Chief Minister said "Because he is a good officer I have taken him to my District". Then I was shifted to Shimoga.

Belgaum experience strengthened my belief that participatory development is the most important approach towards enabling communities to help themselves and sustain efforts in development work.

□

Igniting Minds for Togetherness

Formation of 'Apnadesh Association' in Belgaum in December 1991

My posting in Belgaum proved to be a turning point both in the process of development and in my career. The instrument, which emerged for that turn was Apnadesh Association, the voluntary organisation that we formed there. While looking after the Zilla Parishad work, I found that a large number of activities were there, but the involvement of public was disappointing. People demanded works, which were not a part of the action plan. It indicated that there were genuine demands for work, but the right work was not being selected during the planning and preparation of the action plan.

Involving People in Governance

Conceptually, all of us say that people should be involved in developmental process, but in practice it does not happen that way. I wondered why it was not happening. During a night in the first week of December, I could not sleep properly. Somehow, I tried to sleep, but got up early at 1.00 am itself. I was thinking how people's involvement should be strengthened in governance, how can we motivate people to join hands with the government and how government funds can properly be spent with full transparency and accountability. Then clicked the idea of having a formal structured organisation which is duly registered, under whose banner we organise the people. I discussed the idea with experts the very next day. Finally, we decided to form an Association under the Societies Act. This is how Apnadesh came into being in 1991.

Voluntary Efforts from People

We started meeting every week involving officers and like-minded people voluntarily. During discussions, lots of ideas and suggestions came up in the course of the brainstorming. Some people suggested the starting of coaching in hostels, while some suggested that focus be on plantation in the city. This is how many activities formally began on the ground. Gradually, we received hundreds of demands from public and school betterment committees, expressing willingness to contribute voluntarily. We encouraged that. Apart from the sanctioned budgeted cost of work, I kept about 10% funds for such activities. When people came forward, we issued funds from that pool. It increased confidence of the people—they started contributing and we too started sanctioning new projects.

Resolving Drinking Water Scarcity

In the beginning itself we got two good opportunities to motivate people for voluntary works. One was Fort Kere. When I sanctioned the scheme of Rs. five lakh for making an island in the Tank and restoring it, we gave a public call for *shramdan*. To our surprise, hundreds of NGOs came forward to get registered. We had to give them time slots in shifts. That created a lot of visibility for Apnadesh as well as other NGOs. Then drinking water problem was there in Hukeri. There too the NGOs and people from neighbouring areas started working together. Then we went to other areas like Bhoj and other towns like Chikodi where too drinking water problem was an issue. The activities were multifarious.

Mobilising for Collectiveness

The prime concept of Apnadesh since its inception has been to transform the thinking of people from 'I' to 'We'—thinking about the community work and not self alone. Hence, we began from changing the mindset. It not only created awareness but also enhanced the civic sense among people who started relating to the activities. Whosoever came in our contact was exhorted to ask a question to him/her—what is my contribution? We take everything from the society, but what do we give back to it? People gradually started asking that question to themselves. That way we could motivate people. Initially, when we told people to do something voluntarily, they hesitated saying nothing could be done without money. But, we proved that without money lot of work can be done. If there is donors' contribution, much can be done. Even if there is no monetary contribution one can contribute.

Maintaining Flexibility

Before being a part of the Apnadesh, I took formal permission from the government to take part in such social activities so that there is no controversy at any stage. As an NGO we could have collected donations, but we decided not to do that for Apnadesh. That is why we remained free from any controversy. We never accepted any government grant or participated in any government scheme directly taking funds from the government or anybody else. We do not offer any membership or take any membership fee. We don't believe in formally structuring the organisation. We believe whosoever wants to work should work. They can work individually, collectively or with the government. We have maintained that flexibility. People welcomed this structure. That is why we worked with the government, NGOs and like-minded people. That is why the organisation survived so long. In many areas, we were not in touch of any volunteer, but when we spoke to the people many got inspired. They continued to work in that area depending on their capacity. I am surprised to see that even after a gap of about 25 years we still find people working in many rural areas. It is a very important point.

Developing the Sense of Belonging

Developing the sense of belonging, collectivity and togetherness is a major contribution of Apnadesh. Another advantage is that good quality work happens on the ground, leakages are minimal and limitations of the Officers are understood by the public. The Officers also become responsive to the public. The parties with vested interests, such as contractors, may not be interested in such activities, but all other people come forward wholeheartedly. Desire to do something for the society is there in everyone, what is needed is just ignition. The advantage of working collectively is tremendous. This is what Apnadesh has shown. Today Apnadesh is a household name in many parts of Karnataka. It has produced many trendsetters who are working in their respective areas without seeking any publicity. Pure selfless service.

□

Apnadesh Association

Turning the 'I' feeling' into 'We' feeling

Apnadesh Association is the platform that actually brought general public and the administration together for creating a better society and ensuring genuine public participation in the planning and implementation of government schemes. It is the voluntary organisation that has set high standards in selfless social service and successfully turned the 'I' feeling into the 'We' feeling, something which is regarded by many as unbelievable.

Meaning of 'Apnadesh'

The word 'Apnadesh' has been derived from two Hindi words 'Apna' meaning 'ours' and 'Desh' meaning 'country' or the place to which one belongs. Therefore, it means 'Our Country' or 'the place to which we belong'. It may also mean anything from our family to neighbourhood, block, district, state, nation and the world *'Vasudhaiva Kutumbakam'* (world is a family).

Apnadesh aims at containing 'selfishness' as well as 'ego' and seeks to promote selflessness and sense of giving and sacrifice for larger good of the society. Apnadesh is a symbol of goodness for all. There is no scope for selfishness and personal gain. It fundamentally goes against the basic instinct of life. Seeking pleasure for self is a basic instinct, which drives most people to do everything for themselves only. Most of the struggle throughout the life is basically for self. This is basic animal psychology. But humans are different. They are gregarious and exist in groups having common goals and objectives for which all come together. It is basically the 'We' feeling, which binds different persons/ souls together like a thread of a garland. This is what 'Apnadesh' stands for.

Justification and Need

Today, non-governmental organisations (NGOs) are mushrooming everywhere. Every organisation claims to do 'good' for humanity. Much has been said about charity—'charity begins at home', 'example is better than precept', 'lead by example', 'where there is a will there is a way' and so on. Every voluntary organisation has its own strength and weaknesses too, yet it thinks that it provides the best solution to the problems being faced by the society. Even then most of the NGOs or the people associated with them prefer to move alone. It happens because of the personality clash or due to any hidden agenda.

But Apnadesh does not believe in moving alone. It acts as an umbrella organisation for all the voluntary organisations for the individuals who believe in doing something good to the country or humanity anywhere, anytime. It also stresses that for doing anything good one does not require any group, NGO or institution. What is required is strong will, determination and the intent to do good.

When it comes to do anything good for the society the important question, which confronts us is of resources. The general belief is that for doing anything good one needs resources. But Apnadesh firmly believes that resources don't matter at all. There are over 100 activities, which can be undertaken without any money. All these activities are highly paramount for strengthening the social fabric. What is required is the involvement of the people alone.

Some of the activities, which do not require money, are as follows:

1. **Total Literacy:** Conducting literacy classes to make the village 100% literate. If people come together and take a decision, it is not a difficult task to achieve. Many such successful experiments have been done by Apnadesh at different places in Karnataka.
2. **Promoting Savings:** Villagers can be educated about importance of saving. Spend what is left after saving, rather than first spend then save what is left.
3. **No Dues Village:** People can be made aware of their duties before they exercise their rights. They should be educated about paying their taxes timely and then expecting in return from the administration. Revenue collected timely is utilised for developmental activities in the villages or the localities in urban areas.
4. **Smaller Families:** Every couple in the village should be motivated to adopt family planning. The beauty of small life is explained.
5. **Identifying the Talents:** Students lagging in studies can be imparted special coaching so that they cope up the difficulties. Talent in extra-curricular activities can also be encouraged and those who have potential should be motivated to participate at state, national or international fora.
6. **Green Clean Village:** People may be motivated for planting different species of trees in their backyards or on land available in the villages. After 2-3 years'

nourishment, the trees cover the entire village with greenery, which is a sign of peace and prosperity.

7. **Litigation-free Village:** Unlike the urban areas, the villages have lesser problems like quarrels, fighting, etc. They can be enlightened to sort out the differences within the village itself rather than going to the police station or the court, which make them financially and socially weak.
8. 'Shramdan' **Culture in Village:** The old culture of '*shramdan*' (self-help through voluntary labour) has to be revived and villagers can be mobilised and motivated to participate in weekly '*shramdan*' for any of the activities. It can be conducted on any day.
9. **Donors' Village:** Identify the donors and convince them to help in ensuring basic amenities in villages like building schools, hospitals, Anganwadis, etc. The contribution from donors should be recognised and they should be rewarded suitably in public.
10. **Smoke-free Village:** Installation of biogas plants and improved stoves can be opted for minimising the pressure on the forests. People should be educated about the side effects of smoking and deforestation.
11. **Bonded and Child Labour-free Village:** Helping the District Administration identify bonded and child labour is the collective responsibility. Rehabilitation of the rescued children or people is also important. Awareness campaigns should be conducted to effectively curb bonded and child labour.
12. **Healthy and Hygiene:** Educating people about general well-being of individuals, proper nutrition, periodical health check-up, regular exercise,

adequate rest, positive thinking, clean and hygienic surrounding are the tasks that should be taken up effectively.

13. **Active Voters' Village:** No political party should take the villagers for granted. They should exercise their valuable vote confidently to the deserving candidate who can respond to their difficulties. Once the election process is over and whichever party comes to power, the villagers should take advantage of that for development of the village. The unity displayed during elections should be maintained after the polls too.
14. **Mass Marriage Village:** To curtail unnecessary expenditure on wedding ceremonies and festivals, people can be educated about the advantages of mass marriage.
15. **Complete Pucca Village:** Every house of the village should be pucca. Therefore, identification of the thatched roof houses can be done and efforts can be put to convert them into pucca.
16. **Plastic-free Village:** Plastic being non-degradable is dangerous for all living beings. People should properly be oriented for complete eradication of plastic, thereby declaring the village as Zero Plastic Village.
17. **Alcoholic-free Village:** Since alcohol ruins the family, people have to be educated about its disastrous impact on health and socio-economic condition of an individual and their families.
18. **Confidence-Building among Peasants:** For some time the farmers are unfortunately seen committing suicide for various reasons. They find a solution to their all problems in suicide, which is wrong. Confidence building measures should be taken to instill hope among the people who are in distress.

19. **ICT Village:** The Information and Communication Technology (ICT) should be used for rural transformation. No village should be deprived of the benefits of technological advancements. Educated unemployed youth should be imparted basic computer training so that the people in the village have access to all information necessary for their life. The ultimate objective should be providing urban facilities to rural areas (PURA).

No Collection of Donation

Apnadesh is a unique organisation, which does not believe in collection of funds or donation. It believes that if there is a need the people should collect resources themselves and use them for the common good. There is no membership for anyone. Any person or group can associate themselves with it anytime and anywhere for any good cause. Such flexibility is there. We can do a good work every day at an individual level or in a group. Even though flexibility is there, Apnadesh expects every volunteer to do one good work a day. All the good souls who have good intent and do things for others selflessly are volunteers of Apnadesh, which believes that goodness and badness both are within us. However, it varies in percentage in everyone. Apnadesh intends to increase the ratio of goodness up to the maximum possible level.

Foundation of 'Apnadesh'

When was 'Apnadesh' born is a question. The ideals of Apnadesh are universal and have existed since times immemorial. Formally, Apnadesh was launched in December 1991 at Belgaum District of Karnataka where it was formally registered as an Association. The aims and objectives are noble. Yet the volunteers can work to fulfill any of them individually or in a group. Apnadesh does not prescribe what to do and what not, rather it believes that someone can take a lead in organising the like-minded people, who are in plenty yet invisible. Apnadesh also strongly believes that society exists because of the good people. If what is generally reported at front pages of the newspapers was true, the world would have come to an end so far. The world is full of good souls. What is really needed is the right way to look at them. What is really required is an initiative and motivate others to join that like a thread in a garland. Good people feel suffocated at the happenings around them. They want to assert goodness. They need to be organised. Apnadesh firmly believes in positive actions.

When well-intended people join hands with the Government or an institution, the following positive outcomes are bound to come out:

- A sense of belongingness at all levels
- A sense of togetherness, the 'WE' feeling
- Most effective deployment and use of the resources
- Accountability and transparency is essentially visible
- Positivism spreads and negativity gets eliminated
- Donation motivates the people and also brightens the prospects of future donations for common good
- Disputes disappear, collectivity gets strengthened
- Social harmony strengthens
- Public and government officials come together and understand each other better

Essentials of 'Apnadesh' Activities

- A volunteer should have a spark within him/her
- Voluntarism is not something which can be imposed by others. It can be done selflessly and without boasting about it
- Choice of activities at local level

- Stress on the activities, which do not cost money/ resources
- Volunteers should never accept donations. They should advice the willing participants to form their own group to manage and transparently account them
- 5% resources should be earmarked and used for Apnadesh objectives /activities
- Opinion of the people who matter be documented.
- The good works being done by others or by individuals, institutions should also be documented
- Volunteers should be models for others in every respect
- Reward for good deeds should not be expected, yet it would defiantly come out in the form of lasting peace, happiness of which most others are starved and deprived.

Mission of Apnadesh is very relevant and is needed more than ever before. We must not expect anyone to save us from bad things happening around us. We must take initiative to do whatever is possible within our means. By doing our bit, we would be returning the heavy debt of the motherland on all of us. The earlier we do the better it is.

The change in people's mindset for collective actions is now a reality. It is visible in innumerable villages, cities, towns, and even metro cities of Karnataka through different activities. It has impacted over one lakh rural citizens and is evident in over 3,000 documented success stories. There are people even in remote villages, who instead of waiting for the government agencies for minor developmental activities, come together, take a decision, contribute from their own pockets and finish the work through *shramdan*. In order to strengthen this feeling across the country, Apnadesh has collaborated with over 200 like-minded voluntary organisations. The partnerships are expanding with more and more change agents signing up to better the world around them, readying Apnadesh to merge national and international borders towards garnering equitable living.

It is important that people take it upon themselves to see change around them. If the onus to keep a place clean or save energy is upon the people, then they would definitely take pride in themselves, as they have been the key stakeholders of this development. This is the essence of Apnadesh.

□

SOCIAL AUDIT: NARROWING THE GAP BETWEEN VISION AND REALITY

Social Audit has emerged as an effective way of ensuring quality work and curbing corruption in government schemes. The concept, though still not much popular in India, is surely a way to narrow the gap between the vision and the reality and between efficiency and effectiveness. It allows to measure, verify, and report on how to improve the social performance of any government effort. Conceptually, it goes beyond the realm of traditional financial audit, as it focuses on issues such as awareness, grievance redress and feedback about the programmes.

Pioneered by Charles Medawar in 1972, social audits in India were first made statutory in a 2005 Rural Employment Act and the government issued the Social Audit Rules in 2011 under the MGNREGA Act. The Government says that only ten states viz. Andhra Pradesh, Chhattisgarh, Gujarat, Karnataka, Mizoram, Sikkim, Telangana, Tamil Nadu, Tripura and Uttar Pradesh have operationalised social audit units as laid down in the Social Audit Rules 2011 and states of Madhya Pradesh, Odisha, Manipur, Meghalaya, Rajasthan and Jammu & Kashmir are in the process of doing it.

The Comptroller and Auditor General (CAG) of India on April 13, 2015 instructed all Auditor Generals (AGs) in states to institutionalise social audits and collect district level data on various social sector schemes. The problem with most Indians is that even after 50 years of Independence they do not understand the concept of 'government for the people, of the people, and by the people'. Most people still think themselves as being ruled by the politicians, while politicians think of themselves as the rulers.

How Transparency Becomes a Buzzword

Chief Secretary, Zilla Parishad, Shimoga from June 1992 to April 1994

Shimoga, where I was posted as Chief Secretary of Zilla Parishad in 1992, was a very different experience all together. Politically, Shimoga is very active. It has been a hot bed of many political and social movements. Mr. S. Bangarappa, Kamappa Gordiappa and many other senior politicians have been from this region. Mr. D.B. Chandre Gowda represented it in the Assembly when I was posted there. He served as Speaker of the State Assembly. Then Leader of Opposition Mr. Bookanakere Siddalingappa Yeddyurappa popularly known as B.S. Yeddyurappa, who later became Chief Minister of the state, is also from this region. In those days, Mr. Serekoppa Bangarappa (S. Bangarappa) was the Chief Minister. Mr. Jayadevappa Halappa Patel (J.H. Patel) was another strong leader from the region. I think the land of Shimoga has produced quite a number of Chief Ministers in Karnataka.

Land of Raitsanga Movement

The District is amalgamation of different cultures. In some Talukas, like Teerthahalli, Hosanagra, Sagara, etc. one sees the influence of Malnads. Then in Chandagiri one sees the culture of plane region. Culturally too, it is very developed area. It is also the birthplace of Rashtrakavi Kuvempu. The region has produced lots of leaders in every field. Shimoga is also known for many other things. Raitsanga movement started from here. I got the opportunity to interact with some of the stalwarts of that movement.

When I joined, there was no elected representative in the Zilla Parishad. In those days, the total literacy movement was at the peak. Therefore, it was a real challenge for me to make a difference. In that situation, I was the central person heading all the Departments. Zilla Parishad was the main agency under which all the development projects fell. I took up this challenge in real spirit. I was perfectly armed with the experience of Belgaum—how the officers were, what they do, what they don't do, etc. I was aware of the entire mechanism deeply. That proved very handy for me. That is why when I came to Shimoga I started working from day one. It was like continuing the experience of Belgaum—moving forward and firing all the cylinders. I started touring the district extensively, interacting with people, holding meetings, making perspective plans at Gram Panchayat level, ensuring social audit of the work done and continuing the 'Apnadesh' concept. I interacted with some very progressive farmers also there.

By and large a lot of learning and working happened—working with various departments, bringing harmony in the administration, ensuring coordination, motivating the staff, etc. In every sense of the word in working, my experience was very fulfilling and enriching.

Planning from the Below and Social Audit

Since the elected body was not there, we had to own up various responsibilities—preparation of plans, their timely and effective execution, etc. In the beginning, I did extensive inspection. I made it a point that I would visit all the villages of the District. I also experimented with the concept of planning from below level, in the bottom-up approach as well as with starting social audit. I told the officers to prepare a list of the ongoing and completed works. We formed various teams involving officers and along with those teams we visited the Gram Panchayats. In those meetings, we also invited the former Zilla Parishad members, Gram Panchayat members and even the village elders. And in front of them, the Officers read out the list of the on-going and recently completed works. Then we solicited the opinion of the public about those works. In some cases, they said the work was indeed done, while in some cases they said 'not done, quality not good' or pointed out to some shortcomings. Whatever they said was properly recorded. We did it because it was impossible for the supervisors to visit all the sites. If you present the information in front of the people, they give their frank opinion. If quality is poor, they said quality is not good. If the work was not done they said the work was not done. The work under question was inspected again by the team of officers. We did it in all the Gram Panchayats. I also attended some of the meetings. ACs, Tehsildars, etc all attended the meetings. We also used those fora to illicit the views of the public about future requirements of the villages. We listed the works according to their priorities. That became a planning activity. It was highly successful experiment. In addition to this, we continued the total literacy campaign. We encouraged the volunteers about it. Lot of awareness was generated in the entire district. The officers motivated the public. Some retired persons and NGOs also joined the activities.

Social audit enables the contractor or the implementing agency to take a close look at itself and understand how far it has lived up to its social objectives. It encourages greater concern for social performance. Social audit strengthens local democracy as well as genuine community participation. It hugely benefits disadvantaged sections and promotes collective decision making and sharing responsibilities.

School Betterment Committees

There was huge demand for new works and the public was willing to contribute. Since I had some discretionary fund, I sanctioned those works under that head. The work became so effective that one can still see the school betterment committees in some areas. People in those days took raw material from us and used on their own. Some of the schools did a wonderful job. They undertook huge plantation activities and after some years received good revenue for the village and school betterment by cutting those trees down. It became a big movement. Many people started coming to us to work in PPP mode. We integrated the government resources. Energetic people started work with their own funds and the government fund was provided at later stage. In every village, we publicly displayed the work being done to ensure transparency.

Additionally, we also desilted tanks and did plantation in a big way. Village forest committees were also activated. The details of the government schemes were painted on the walls. Donors' boards were also installed. This not only brought the public and government machinery together, but also generated the sense of contributing voluntarily among the common masses.

Coming together surely makes a difference. If there is more transparency in government functioning the people trust the agencies and extend active help. Secrecy develops skepticism that must be avoided. Lack of transparency results in distrust and a deep sense of insecurity. When we open the door toward openness and transparency, a lots of people follow you through.

□

DONATION FOR NATION

'Shramdan' *has been part of Indian ethos since time immemorial, but the model of governance that we have followed during all these decades after Independence pushed the voluntary efforts in the back, and the mindset of depending upon the government machinery for everything got strengthened. As the government interference in rural development increased, the people there too started distancing themselves from voluntary efforts. As a result, a major part of government budget for any project goes into payment of labour.*

Realising the significance of the age old tradition of shramdaan, *Prime Minister Narendra Modi, in his* 'Mann ki Baat' *address on September 25, 2016, appealed to the people to devote a few hours for Swachh Bharat Abhiyan. On his call, people in various parts joined the cleanliness drive. There can be a thousand ways to contribute—volunteering at homeless shelters, planting trees in the neighbourhood, cleaning streets, offering a seat in the train to someone who needs it more than us, opening doors for others, donating food, clothing and other material goods to homeless shelters, disaster relief, animal shelters, etc. A dirty spot, a garbage dump, a polluted lake or anything can be changed with a little effort. But the big question is how to motivate people for it. They generally do not respond to the call by a corrupt politician or officer. But, if the Officer or the leader is honest and makes sincere efforts, then the people definitely respond. This is what we witnessed in Shimoga, Karnataka, during the nineties when thousands of people voluntarily whitewashed 1,200 government buildings in a single day on January 26.*

Amazing Results of Public-Private Partnership

Maintenance of public buildings and fencing of government lands are big tasks in government functioning. In Shimoga, lots of requests came to me for it when I was Chief Secretary of Zilla Parishad. The expenses on such works are so huge that the normal grants prove insufficient. When we estimated the work in the district, we found it would require many crores of rupees. It was difficult to arrange that much amount at that time. Therefore, we planned to do that work with a difference. We decided to whitewash all rooms of the schools and the government buildings including the roadside bus shelters on a single day i.e. on January 26.

Shramdan for Whitewashing 1200 Public Buildings in a Single Day

The planning in this regard began in the month of December. First, we listed the schools and other public buildings. Then we estimated the quantity and cost of the lime to be required. We asked the officials to buy lime in sufficient quantity and pack it in small boxes with clear instructions depending upon the size of the building, as is done during the election time. A weak ahead, we handed over those boxes to the persons concerned with the request to mobilise local people on January 26 for performing *shramdan* after the flag hoisting ceremony. To our surprise, we found that in the entire district on that single day alone more than 1,200 public buildings were whitewashed. All teachers, staff members, public, youth and women voluntarily joined the initiative with full enthusiasm. It became big news in the district. The work, which was going to cost crores of rupees, was done in a few lakh rupees only. We had to spend money on the material alone and it fetched a new look to the public buildings in a single day's time.

Revolutionising the Voluntary Service

There are many other things that we did in the District. For wildlife preservation lot of work was done. Singhdhama, which is close to Shimoga, was given lots of funds for development as a tourist spot. Though it comes under the Forest Department, the Zilla Parishad also helps it. Apart from it, we activated the School Betterment Committees. Our motivation made them very accountable. Meanwhile, many small milk societies also approached us for funds. Since the milk societies are self-sustaining, there was no scheme for their help. Even then, we granted them some funds to encourage them. Similarly, we also granted funds for Anganwadi buildings.

The voluntary activities emerged as a parallel department in the district. In such activities Total Literacy Campaign was on top. Shimoga then was ahead of all the Districts in implementation of the existing government schemes like Ashraya, Vishwa, IRDP, etc. Ashraya had begun then only. Vishwa was for technical skill upgradation. The plan was to construct a work shed in each Gram Panchayat. Lots of works started under that scheme. The activities in Shimoga for both development and public participation became a landmark in the state. It was reported widely not only by the local press, but also by the state press. State presspersons studied the whole concept and published the details. It was at that time that 'Apnadesh' was recognised by a group of people and Sir Vishveshwaraiah Award was conferred on it.

Public Monitoring of Developmental Projects

This is a fact that major projects can be executed only by the government, because the government can spend huge money on any big project like drinking water project, construction of big barrages, construction of big roads, etc. Public cannot participate in these activities beyond a certain limit. It is the category of work where public involvement is least. There is second category of work, which does not cost much, but people can get involved in them. If any big building or road is sanctioned in an area the people do not need to contribute in construction work, but supervision can be done by them. They can form a committee to check whether the work is being done properly, contractor is working properly or not. That involvement of people forms a part of 'Apnadesh' activities. Government does the funding, but the public can also participate.

Activities That Require No Money

There is third category of works, which do not cost money. Generally, people believe that nothing can be done without money. But, our experience shows that there are so many works, which can be done without money. Building a sense of community or brotherhood happens when people work together for a common cause. That is what we did in Shimoga. We identified the number of activities, which can be done by individuals, groups and voluntary organisations, because money is not required for them. These are the works, which are necessary for any society. Rather these are the real nation-building activities. Spreading literacy, generating awareness about family planning, opening savings bank accounts, plantation of saplings, helping each other, resolution of local disputes, prohibition, adoption of family planning measures, etc, require individual motivation. If one indulges in consumption of liquor, its needs to be curbed at individual level. The government cannot force one to stop it. But for such activities neither government resources are required, nor money.

Minimising the Leakage

That is what is done by Apnadesh. It concentrates on the last two categories of works. Once, the people interact with us, they get involved. That we did successfully in Shimoga. Fact is that if the public is not involved in government projects, the works are executed through the contractors only—you issue tender, find out the agency, they do the work and you pay for it. In such activities, the quality of work is left to the Department personnel only. But when we involve people, their supervision can minimise leakages. They do not allow substandard work. They realise that the project once finished will cater to their needs only. If care is not taken, it is they who shall suffer. The way it is done at our own homes, it has to be done in public also.

Bringing the Officials Closer to Community

The joint efforts between the government and the public strengthen fraternity among the employees and public. It helps the public understand the genuine problems of the officers and officers understand the public sentiments. It brings the like-minded people together. These are the benefits of public participation initiatives. The thing that we have noticed during all these years is that the public does not participate unless they feel for that work and unless officer is committed. Public may have feeling for the work, but if the officer is not motivated, they will not come forward. The Public is very sharp, they know the difference between what is good and what is bad. If your efforts are genuine, they come together and that togetherness sometimes creates history.

□

Mangalore: India's Singapore in Waiting

Deputy Commissioner and District Magistrate, Dakshin Kannada District, Mangalore, from April 1994 to July 1996

Considering its geographical location, Mangalore city has all the potential to grow as the second big city in Karnataka after Bengaluru. It has port, air and rail connectivity. Not only this, three national highways also pass through it. Konkan Railway is also there. Despite so much connectivity and even high levels of education and awareness among the local people, the town has not grown to its full potential both industrially and commercially. It has huge potential to develop as a major coastal town on the lines of Honking, Singapore, etc. But, unfortunately it has not been developed to its full potential due to various reasons.

Averting Communal Clash

During my tenure in 1994, the major project, which was coming up near the city was Mangalore Refinery and Petrochemical Limited (MRPL). Land acquisition was taking place. But, lot of agitation was engineered by some people opposing the project. Once the fishermen too gave a call for a bandh. They came out of their houses and blocked the NH 17, which runs along the coast—coming from Kerala and going up to Goa. Back then Udupi was also a part of Mangalore. The Administration tried to rein in the protestors through slight lathicharges, etc. But some leaders of the fishermen, along with some MLAs started staging a dharna in front of the DC Office. The whole day passed like this. In afternoon around 3.30 pm, I came to know that some people had thrown *'chappals'* (slippers) at a religious place behind the DC Office. Since agitation was already going on, in that situation if a communal clash had developed it could have taken a dangerous turn. I immediately dispatched police officials to the fishermen leaders inviting them for dialogue. They came after some time. The SP was also sitting there. I shouted at the fishermen leaders saying people are suffering because of your agitation. You have registered your protest, so now call it off. They said they could not do that. I said your time is up. You people have thrown *'chappals'* at the religious place and we are going to book you for attempting to incite communal violence. They got scared and said they had not done that. We said only you are responsible for the tense situation. Better, you call off the agitation, otherwise be ready to go to the jail. Finally, they agreed to call off the agitation. We put them in an open police jeep and gave a mike. They went on announcing that the agitation was called off from the DC office itself. Finally, the highway was cleared.

Huge Potential, Poor Development

Like this, we faced so many agitations. Some environmental groups were also agitating against industrialisation. Problem is that people discriminate against even the positive industrialisation. Opposition to polluting industries can be understood but you cannot oppose every industry. After all, industries generate employment. People migrate from Mangalore in search of jobs. If industries are there in the city itself, local people will get more employment. But they continued the agitation. Sometimes we have to deal with a few such protesters sternly. What

I want to say that the town has so much population and potential, but it is not getting developed which is a very sad thing. It should develop and become a hub of activities.

In addition to the fishermen activities we had the Paryaya festival in Udupi. The change of Swamiji happens there. Big festival takes place. In Udupi, we had planned to widen the main road, which goes to Manipal. We had even marked the widening sign—how much area to be widened. Some people started interfering. They wanted to agitate. They questioned what were we doing, and put that in cold storage. Later, the road was widened subsequently when it became a separate district.

Master Plan for City

At that time we had prepared a Master Plan for Mangalore—Greater Mangalore Plan. I integrated futuristic things—how the city would develop in next 25 years. We had planned the growth of Mangalore up to Mulki, BC Road, University Area. We had planned that as greater region. However, during my tenure it could not be fully materialised. We did lots of other activities too. Disposal of old papers, pendency reduction, development of Pilikula, disposal of old cases like the revenue cases, etc. were undertaken on a large scale. At that time there were highest number of land Tribunal cases. People remember Mr. S.K. Das for land reforms.

Consciousness about Rights

Once a very strange thing happened. I was sitting in the Office. One visitor came and sat in front of me. He asked me if I was the registering authority for newspapers. I said, yes. He said I wish to register a complaint. I asked him what the complaint was. He said, today my vender did not deliver the newspaper. I have subscribed it, but the vender has discontinued it without providing any notice. I laughed internally. Even then, I said if you did not get the newspaper you don't pay him money for one day. He said no, no, if the newspaper is printed, I should have the news. Because it did not come, I am deprived of the news. It shows how people are conscious and aware of their rights.

In Mangalore, the people do not like ringing up to the politician. They say you dispose it of. Take whatever decision you like, but dispose it of as soon as possible. It is a good thing. They want the matter should not linger on. Another good thing is that the MLAs there did not complain of the work given to other MLAs. They say give work to me also. In other areas, people fight over the work given to others and they even try to get it cancelled. The political maturity is much more in Mangalore. It is worth emulating.

□

When Road Widening Became a Movement

After transfer from Shimoga, I joined as Deputy Commissioner (DC) in Mangalore in 1994. The job of DC, as compared to the previous postings, was a different one because the DC is overall in-charge of the Administration. He is also the spokesperson of the state government at District level. So, all the issues and things converge at that level and the DC has to provide leadership in every situation whether it is maintenance of law and order, development, coordination among various departments, conduct of elections, fighting the calamities, etc.

Land of Enterprising People

Mangalore is a uniquely placed district where the literacy rate, both among men and women, was the highest in the state, telephone connectivity was highest and large numbers of people from here migrated to Gulf countries, Mumbai or other places across the country. People are quite enterprising there. Five banks originated from Dakshin Kannada only. It is a port city having three national highways and the Konkan Railway passes through it too.

In that matrix, when I was posted, I constantly visualised what to do. At that time, I was also holding the charge of Zilla Panchayat, Corporation and various other institutions. I thought I should do something different. So, I started analysing the things. One of the main problems in the city was of terrible roads. After every rainy season, the condition of road would become worse. Traffic congestion in several areas, very narrow roads, lots of private buses plying on the city roads were there too. The density of buses was too high. More buses plying on the same route left very less space for the pedestrians and small vehicles. In that situation, I thought of the idea of widening the roads and also finding the permanent solution to those bad roads.

Discipline Comes from the Top

The first thing that we did was to start widening the roads from public places and near the government offices. Because we did not require to ask anybody for it. We shifted the boundary walls behind. Many educational institutions are there too. We requested them to part their lands. Some agreed quickly on requesting them personally on the condition that the Administration would do the civil work, for which we too agreed. That is how we started the work. When some institutions agreed, the remaining institutions also had to agree. We took up the road leading to Port side, in front of the Corporation area. We started acting against the under-construction buildings where norms were being violated. Those who had committed minor violations were asked to contribute in development of roads and footpaths in front of their houses. They came forward for it. For beautification, some advertisers came forward to sponsor the works.

In a short period of six months it became a sort of movement. The situation was that you asked people, and they responded positively. I was also surprised with the response of the people in that area. Because, one can see in Dakshin Kannada that people are highly oriented and are aware of their rights, they do not give up easily. When you ask them to part with land (the most precious thing for an individual human being) they were not easily ready for that without compensation. In those days, the TDR concept was also not there. But in our case, they were ready for it too. The only reason was that we were asking for the public cause. The response was overwhelming. In some of the areas like in Wenlock Hospital and public institutions areas we took land for road widening. In one case I got a call from the Health Secretary questioning us for taking the hospital land. I said I have taken it for the public cause and not for my personal use. Since it is located here, we had to take land from here only and not from anywhere else. We built the wall and went ahead without even waiting for the formal orders from them. That is how we could decongest the place.

Shifting of the Bus Stand

The congestion problem at the Private Bus stand at Hampankatta was very serious. Taking strong action, we dug the road leading to the Bus stand at night and stopped everything. Then they called a strike and stropped plying the buses. We engaged the private vehicles. After a few hours, they reconciled and resumed the work. Then we went ahead in shifting the bus stand. Since it was temporary thing the buses kept on plying in a circular way. It did not stop completely.

Pressure from Transporters

The bus lobby was very strong. They tried to get us pressurised immensely. But in those days, I literally stopped picking up the phone calls till we finished the work. But after some time they realised the intention. Many of the bus owners also agreed that the widening of the road was required and a permanent bus stand is required too. But they were not ready to go to the alternate bus stand. The land near the present Corporation Office that has been given to the Infosys was to be used for bus stand. There was a nine-acre land where we wanted this alternative arrangement to take place. However, it could then be materialised, and we could streamline the traffic. Even today after so much expansion of the city, one does not find congestion there. We did not ask for any state or central funds for it. The whole work was done with the local support. We engaged the local people and agencies and even built the concrete roads.

□

DEATHS IN POLICE CUSTODY

Death in police custody is a sensitive matter that puts the entire law enforcing machinery on the defensive. The matter, if not handled cautiously, earns the entire system a bad name. According to National Crime Records Bureau (NCRB), India annually witnessed 98 deaths in police custody between 2001 and 2013. NCRB records reveal that 1,275-people died in police custody between 2001 and 2013, but less than 50% of custodial deaths led to a case being registered. The deaths in judicial custody—or in prisons—as reported by National Human Rights Commission (NHRC) are much higher. About 12,727 people are reported to have died in judicial custody between 2001 and 2010.

Maharashtra, Andhra Pradesh and Gujarat had the most custodial deaths during 2001-2013, while Bihar reported only six such cases. Among the larger states, Haryana filed a case for every custodial death during the period. The states of Manipur, Jharkhand and Bihar also registered cases for 100% of custodial deaths, but they had reported only two, three and six deaths, respectively. In comparison, Maharashtra registered cases for only 11.4% of the custodial deaths. The possibility of police officers being convicted dwindles at the chargesheeting stage itself—34 policemen are chargesheeted for every 100 cases registered, and only 12% of the chargesheeted policemen are convicted. The Prevention of Torture Bill, passed by Lok Sabha in 2010, has now lapsed. Apart from the effective legal provisions, sensitisation of the entire machinery is required to curb the custodial deaths.

Dealing with Death in Police Custody

During my posting in Mangalore, there was an incident of lock-up death in Kundapur, a coastal town. As we received the information at night, I, along with the SP rushed to the Police Station. The situation was very tense. People had gheraoed the Police Station. That whole night we were in the Police Station. We tried to contact the local MLA, but he was not there. Somehow, we traced him and requested to pacify the locals. As the dead body was taken to hospital for a postmortem, thousands of people gathered there too. They were not ready to trust the doctors of the hospital and insisted on postmortem by outside doctors. We agreed to that and arranged doctors from Udupi. The postmortem was done and the postmortem report also came. But the crowed was still sthere, shouting slogans against the Police. They wanted to attack the Police Station and the Hospital. The youth, who died in the lock-up, was the only bread earner in his family. Police said he had killed himself, but the public did not believe the story. Finally, the MLA arrived and he spoke to the crowd and then they returned home. This is how we controlled the situation.

Acting with Patience

Such incidents take place when we do not take precautions. Any death in Police custody is a serious matter—not only from the human rights angle, but from all angles. In such a situation, managing law and order becomes very difficult, as you cannot resort to lathicharge or adopt any other means to disperse the public. Any minor provocation can make the situation go out of control. We handled the situation very patiently. When someone dies inside a Police Station, the whole administration is seen with suspicion. Even if the head of the administration is fair, people look at him too with an eye of suspicion and feel he/she is supporting the Police or whichever department is accused. Tackling such situations is very difficult, especially its law and order aspect. That is what I learnt.

Death in police custody has always been a challenge for any administrator. This happens everywhere. The administration is supposed to protect the lives of the people and uphold the dignity of law. In case of lock-up death, the entire administration becomes defensive. It loses moral rights to tell the public as to why it happened. Even if they are not at fault, they are still seen with suspicion. That is the very testing time for any administrator.

When the administration itself is on a defensive position, even for the general administrator it becomes very difficult to convince the public. In such cases, all types of angers—individual, collective, old or new, etc.—find expression. That is why it turns more sensitive. That anger does not confine to an individual, rather bursts against the entire department. In such a situation, one has to be very sensitive and patient. Even if there is a provocation—lot of provocation happens at that time—the people handling the situation must not get provoked. Otherwise it may take a different turn. The entire issue gets sidelined and some other issue becomes important. That is how it flairs up.

Common Sense is the Biggest Asset

Since, at that point of time, the public sentiments are running very high, one has to try the best of their common sense. One should involve the community, like the MLA or other influential people, who can come to the rescue of the administration. When the Police are accused, if the person heading the administration has good standing, that also helps. The seniormost person from the police or the general administration should visit the spot immediately, because the presence of the officer itself makes the things easier.

Timely Action Makes Things Easier

In any emergency, the presence of the administration on the spot makes the things easier. If they are absent, the anger increases as to why they are absent. They are accused of being insensitive. That becomes double whammy. If they are on the spot, the people feel the administration is trying its best. They are not at fault. That understanding is very important. I have seen it in many other situations also like floods. During any natural calamity, the administration should reach the spot first. I remember an incident in Mangalore. I got a call from the local MLA at 2.00 am. He informed me about a whirlwind like calamity. I said I would come in the morning. He advised me to come at night itself. I rushed the spot and saw the whole national highway was blocked. The force of the wind was so high that it uprooted everything that came its way. Normally the whirlwind goes in very narrow area, but it destroys everything coming in its way. Not only the trees were uprooted, the tiles from the roofs flew. That caused lot of damage. Because I was awake, we alerted the entire machinery.

Next day, by 11 am when the then Chief Minister Mr. Veerappa Moily visited the spot, almost everything was restored to its original position. Uprooted trees were removed from the highway. Roof tiles were given to the people and they were fixed in the houses. Even compensation was disbursed to the people. In such situation, one cannot repair the total damage, but at least the possible dent to the image of administration can be prevented. In another situation during flood, we carried cash and cheques and disbursed them to the victims on the spot. If you see the damage has happened, you record it and disperse the compensation. If we act faster, the situation becomes less intensive. So, the presence makes difference. In custodial death, too, the presence of the officers makes it easier to handle the situation. The quickness of the response and sincerity help.

In case of death in police custody, when you visit the spot, you can make out whether the death is due to third degree treatment, medical or any other reason. Normally, the hard core criminals do not die of third degree treatment. However, we cannot justify the third degree methods in all cases. In case of the death of a woman, child or a person belonging to the lower strata picked up for any local fight, gives cause for suspicion. Then action has to be taken against the erring policemen. We cannot just leave it. It is nothing but a crime. The persons responsible have to face the consequences. The endeavour should be to achieve balanced level of functioning where police respect human rights, adhere to law and take confidence building measures. □

A Unique Idea of Eco-Tourism
Pilikula Nisargadham, Mangalore

Mangalore, located in the Western Ghats alongside the West coast of India is a bustling port city with a highly educated and aware citizenry and a rich cultural heritage. In spite of being surrounded by the evergreen forests, what was missing was a destination where the people could go and appreciate the natural wealth of the Western Ghats and get educated about its flora, fauna and the rich culture. Besides getting edutainment and learning about the practical aspects of Science, Pilikula Nisargdham emerged as an answer to all these. But more important was converting this grand idea into a reality, which is a lesson in administrative innovation, convergence, synergy, sustainability and public private partnership.

Mangalore: The Heart of the Tulu-land

Mangalore, with about a 0.5 million population is the main port city of Karnataka. It is located about 350 kilometers west of Bangalore. It has the unique distinction of being located between the Arabian Sea and the Western Ghats. It's the headquarters of Dakshin Kannada District. The name Mangalore comes from the local Goddess Mangaladevi. The *Yakshagana,* a night-long dance and drama performance, originated in this region. Kambala, a race involving buffaloes, organised on paddy fields is a major traditional sport here. The people of this city take pride in having one of the highest literacy rates in the country.

It was in the year 1995 when I was Deputy Commissioner of Karwar, I pondered over this issue. It was a coincidence that the State Government issued a circular highlighting the need for setting up large urban lung spaces in major cities. This circular spurred the District Administration into action and the search for a suitable space began. It was though that a unique project, which would provide education, recreation, exposure to nature, feel of the rich cultural heritage of the area would be taken up.

In a district level officers meeting, suggestions came for different locations to set up a multipurpose urban park. It was decided that field visits be made to all these locations. After several inspections, the nursery belonging to the Forest Department measuring about 20 acres located about 11 km away from the city was found suitable. A tough trek through the land and the neighbouring areas covered by bushes and wild growth revealed that a large chunk of land surrounded the nursery and the ownership of these lands was unclear. There were several encroachments apart from a breached tank and an abandoned quarry. During the visit it was revealed that a TB sanatorium existed there. Immediately, I ordered a detailed survey of all the neighbouring lands. While searching the records, it surprisingly came to our knowledge that about 350 acres of lands in that area belonged to the Government. We thought that could be useful for an eco-park in Mangalore.

The available vast land was a virtual goldmine where the potential of the new concept could be explored. But getting the possession of the land was not easy as there were several hutments spread over the land, besides the ownership of land was vested with different governmental agencies. As a first step that I took using my administrative powers under the Land Revenue Act, I reserved the entire chunk of land for a theme park. This immediately put to rest the half-baked proposals of different agencies for different purposes. Thus, it brought in a unity of purpose for the entire piece of land, thereby sowing the seeds for the project.

Immediately, the land was to be protected from any further encroachment or diversion to any other use. Using the funds available under the interest earned on various schemes, a fence was erected around the area.

The Broader Plan

The plan, broadly, was to create a wild life park, a park displaying the flora of the region, an entertainment centre mainly comprising of a water park, a science centre to enable learning with fun and an artisan village to promote the local disappearing arts. The entire land was divided amongst these activities. There was a water body where all the run-off water of the area would get collected. But it was totally breached, silted and encroached. The idea for a wild park came out of compulsion to relocate an old deer park in the city near the Circuit House, which was not sufficiently large to hold the deer. Translating this grand plan onto ground was the next big challenge, we faced.

Designing the Organisational Structure

Such projects, apart from being huge in size, also require continuous monitoring to make them sustainable. An ordinary government type committee would not have worked. Therefore, it was thought that an autonomous structure needs to be put in place. A society was registered with membership from officers and citizens. As the project had several components, a sub-committee for each component was constituted involving the concerned officers and experts from public and eminent citizens. These sub-committees met regularly and developed the ideas further. Each month, a meeting of all the sub-committees together would be convened by the Deputy Commissioner to review the progress and ensure that the projects were moving in right direction.

Ideally speaking, a project of this size should have been implemented at one go, but mobilising the resources was an issue. Therefore it was decided that a step by step approach would be preferable rather than a mega step through which the entire project could be taken up. Various components of the master plan were taken up individually and detailed Project reports prepared for each one of them.

Resources Mobilisation

A project of this dimension required huge amount of funds, which could not have been provided from the limited resources available with the Deputy Commissioner. Therefore, it was decided to split the project into various sub-components such as:

- **Funded Under Regular Government Schemes:** Science Centre as well as a Regional Science Centre was proposed to the Government of India. The project was sanctioned by Government of India. Several components of the recreational activities were funded by the State Tourism Department. Afforestation of the park, planting of trees was approved by the State Forest Department. Nurseries of Forest Department and Horticulture Department, which were located elsewhere, were transferred to this project.
- **Involvement of Private Sector:** The project had a water park as a component. This activity had good revenue generating potential. Therefore, it was thought that it should be entrusted to a professional agency, which would create and run the water park. A transparent procedure was followed to identify an investor and a suitable piece of land was leased for this purpose. Similarly, a golf course was also set up with contributions from the prospective users. In

addition, there was potential of having luxury huts where tourists could stay for longer durations. The Jungle Lodges and Resorts Ltd (A Government of Karnataka Company) was requested to move in and take up this activity.

- **Funds under CSR:** Major companies in the region came forward to take up small components of work of the project such as enclosures for animals, adoption of animals etc. A tank was to be rejuvenated which required massive desilting. Heavy earth moving machinery was made available by a big company and the district administration had to provide the fuel only.

Rehabilitation was a Challenge

Taking possession of the land required shifting of about 250 dwelling units. Those families had unauthorisedly built their houses on that land. An alternate piece of land was identified near the city, sites were formally handed over to the evacuees and houses were built for them under government schemes. The Gram Panchayat was closely involved in survey and rehabilitation work. Care was taken that all the school going children were admitted to the nearby school. A large number of them got employed in the park activities directly or indirectly.

Rejuvenation of Tank

The tank was the centre around which all the activities of the park would revolve. As the tank was located at the lowest point of the park, drains were made from all over the park to channelise the run-off water to this tank. The tank had become totally silted and the side walls had collapsed. The desilting was a major capital intensive activity requiring heavy earth moving equipment. Fortunately, it was discovered that some earth moving equipment was lying idle in a mining company. They were requested to provide the equipment, which they agreed on the condition that the fuel to be provided by the project authorities. The equipment was taken from that company and another company came forward to meet the fuel expenses. By this way, the desilting work was completed. The removed silt was used for tree plantation in another part of the park. The tank was also to be used for recreation purposes. Therefore, a boating jetty was built and paddle boats and rowing and motor boats were introduced.

Biological Park

About 100 acres of land was earmarked for a wildlife park of its own kind. The concept was to keep the animals in large enclosure as per the revised guideline of the Zoo Authority of India. In these big enclosures, the animals would get a feel of being in open spaces rather than being confined in small cages. The enclosures were made by several companies under their CSR. Funds were also obtained from the State Government. The animals came by relocating them from congested zoos. The maintenance of this wild life park is done using the entry fees collected. The staff was provided by the park authority. Some of the zoo animals were adopted by donors.

With all these efforts, Pilikula Biological Park was classified as a Major Zoo by the Central Zoo Authority of India. It is the only zoo recognised as a breeding centre for King Cobras. The park has about 400 animals, reptiles and birds.

Water Park in PPP Mode

Water supply was in abundance in the park because of the high rainfall catchment area. It was thought that a water park would be a major attraction. But since it required huge investment and at the same time it had revenue generating potential, it was decided to entrust this to a private investor.

A long term lease of land was given to the investor, who in turn undertook setting up the park.

Heritage Village

As the traditional arts of the area were fast disappearing, an effort was made to arrest the trend. It was thought that a heritage village be set up in the Pilikula Park where the artisans would stay and work on their arts and display these to the visitors and thereby earn their livelihoods. Apart from the display of their products a separate market outlet was provided in the city. Twenty-five artisan families were moved to the village where they have been working since then. The village has traditional cottages with full-fledged demonstration facilities. Every cottage is dedicated to a particular art form. In addition a 'Guttu Mane' meaning house of the village chief is recreated for the visitors to have a feel of the village life. Furthermore, to showcase the traditional sport of bull racing a 'Kambala field' has been created where live races are held periodically.

Science Centre

The city missed a Science Centre despite being very high in literacy. A Science Centre serves the dual purpose of entertaining people through science experiments on one hand and attracting students towards science learning on the other. This was funded by state funds. Motivated by the success of the science centre, a regional Science Centre was set up with the help of Government of Karnataka and National Council of Science Museums.

Involving Students

To direct the energy of children towards society building activities, the help of the Bharat Scouts and Guides was sought. They were requested to set up a camping site for the students. This was readily done by the project committee and the management of the camping site was taken over by the Dakshin Kannada District Scouts and Guides.

The Challenges Faced

- The project was unique in the sense that it was a combination of entertainment, education, nature conservation and cultural heritage preservation.
- The project was structured in a manner that its success was not dependent on individuals. The structure made the project autonomous and at the same time ensuring its accountability.
- The project is an excellent example of convergence of resources.
- Public participation and Corporate Social Responsibility contributed to the project being sustainable.
- The project is a good example of 'back to the basics' of field inspection, investigation into old records, close supervision and above all transparency and accountability.
- The committees on different components were given sufficient delegation, which ensured the successful completion of each component.
- People's participation right from conceptualisation, implementation and finally in usage made the project irreversible.
- The project is an example as how there can be no conflict amongst various stakeholders if big projects are taken up in right earnestness.

□

Branding the Unexplored
Director, Tourism Department, from August 1996 to September 1997

Karnataka is one of the most important states having so much potential from the tourism point of view. Everything is there for tourists except snow and desert. We have best of wild life, beaches and two world heritage centres. Mysore, as heritage city attracts lots of tourists. Pattadakal and Hampi are world heritage sites. Two popular tourist destinations—Goa and Kerala—are very close by. After taking over as Director of Tourism Department in 1996, I realised that despite having so much tourism potential the branding of the state is not much. The other states market their destinations very much. Goa is already a well-known destination. Kerala is also coming up in a big way, as the state has been very aggressive in its tourism branding and marketing.

Repackaging into Circuits

So, we focused on branding the state in a proper manner. We engaged consultants, redesigned the logo and literature. We introduced the concept of circuit-based literature and information for tourists dividing the tourist places into circuits such as religious circuit, coastal circuit, heritage circuit, wild life circuit, etc. We basically repackaged the things. Incentive based Tourism Policy for hotels, restaurants and new ventures was introduced.

But, the budget provided was very meager. When I came in the Department, the total budget was ₹ 10 crore. After lots of struggles and representations, it was increased by only Rs. two crore in the new budget. Though it was 20% increase compare to the previous year, in totality it was not much. Then we tried to get some funds from the central government, because the then Prime Minister H.D. Deve Gowda was from our State. We pushed our case for funds, but that did not materialise much.

Focus on Publicity and Hygiene

When we introspected and analysed why the state lagged behind in tourism, we found that publicity was inadequate. Our destinations were not well-known outside the state. So, we thought of opening offices in other states and also having an exchange programme or a mutually supportive system with other states. In Delhi, where we have our Information Department and Emporium, we decided to do a lot of improvement. We introduced Kannada food festivals in Delhi. Once we organised such a festival and lots of people came. Our concentration was on getting more funds from the Centre and devising the strategy for circuit wise publicity of our tourist destinations. At the same time, we focused on making the tourist spots cleaner and improving the approach roads leading to them. We wanted PWD Roads in those areas so that whenever people go there, their journey should be comfortable. Health and hygiene are two main concerns of tourists. Therefore, we tried to ensure that.

New Golden Triangle of Goa, Karnataka and Kerala

In those days, we had a progressive Tourism Policy. Considering the limited resources, we couldn't achieve much. However, we could not be as aggressive as other states like Kerala and Rajasthan were. Maximum number of tourists visit Delhi, Agra and Jaipur—the golden triangle.

Here also we thought of having a golden triangle involving Goa, Karnataka and Kerala. If we link these states, it will be a big boost to the tourism. Good access from Goa to Hampi and other destinations could be one option. Hampi is really a magnificent destination. Though it is not well connected, it still attracts thousands of foreign tourists. They come to see and study those sites. The whole place is quite mesmerising.

In Karnataka, we have lots of reservoirs and rivers where water sports can be promoted. Downstream of these reservoirs, lot of land is there, which could be converted into gardens and a support system for tourists. That was in my mind. What we did in Pilikula in Mangalore was also to promote tourism and to create a place for infotainment. That is what our state had to do aggressively.

Tapping the Employment Potential

The employment potential in tourism investment is much more. If you create one employment by investing Rs. one crore in any industry or any other area, you can create ten more employments by investing the same amount in tourism. We need to tap that potential. In some states like Kerala, Goa, and Rajasthan, the income from tourism is the mainstay. But, it is not so in case of Karnataka despite having world class tourist destinations.

At the same time, we emphasised on eco-tourism. We gave lot of support to jungle lodges and resorts. Wherever we received such proposals we supported them. They could renovate their existing infrastructure and also add into the existing infrastructure. Since, the Karnataka State Tourism Development Corporation was not in a good financial position, we tried to support it from the Government. Karnataka has unlimited potential. Mysore's Dussehra festival is well known all over the world. Similarly, Bangalore is well known for education, research and IT.

Huge Potential in Health and Recreation

Other areas, which are coming up fast in tourism

sector, are health and recreation. Coastal areas can also be developed on a large scale. What Kerala has is also available in coastal areas of Karnataka. Agriculture tourism is also possible. Tourists can be taken to farms also to educate them about agriculture activities.

On the whole there are immense possibilities of development. In the time to come if work is done with a vision, Karnataka will become a hot destination. Foreign tourists definitely provide most of the revenue, but at the same time domestic tourists should also not be neglected, as there is big section of domestic tourists who can be turned to Karnataka. Lots of people from West Bengal and Maharashtra go outside everywhere. They can be tapped.

□

Among the Sun and Sand

Deputy Commissioner & District Magistrate of Uttar Kannada District, Karwar, from September 1997 to September 1998

From Tourism Department, I went to Karwar in 1997 as Deputy Commissioner and D.M. It is a beautiful seaside town located on Goa-Karnataka border under Uttar Kannada District. Situated on the Western Coast, the scenic place is blessed with wonderful forests, fascinating natural beauty and the marvellous beaches offering a breathtaking view of its landscape, rugged hills, and clear backwaters. The very view of mountains rising out of the Arabian Sea is mesmerising. Once the headquarters of British Government, Karwar has been the sea trade centre from Arabian Sea and Arabs, Dutch, Portuguese, French and British have traded here historically.

Reasonable Compensation to Fishermen

Since it is mainly a forest district, there were many environmental issues. A nuclear power plant was coming up across the river. Some hydro power projects were also there. The land acquisition process for the sea bird project was going on. Local people were strongly agitating against it. They had their own concerns. One of the major concerns was of low compensation. It was a defence project, but the compensation offered by the officials was indeed low—a few thousand rupees per acre. The agitating fishermen had refused to take it. The problem was really serious and pathetic. The agitating people were not against acquisition of their lands. They said, if it is a defence project, there is no question of opposition, but give us reasonable compensation. Their demand was justified. After studying the whole issue, I explained it to the then Chief Minister Shri J.H. Patel who was astonished to see the way the compensation amount was fixed and declared.

After obtaining CM's permission, I sent the officers to study the Upper Krishna Project (UKP), which had offered a good rehabilitation package. We brought those package details, studied them and then proposed the same in Karwar. What was paid in UKP should be paid here too. We sent the proposal to the state government, which readily agreed. Then we sent the proposal to the Central government. The then Union Defence Minister George Fernandez also visited the project personally and looked into the whole issue. At last, we could succeed in getting reasonable compensation for the people. The agitation against the project gradually became negligible.

Resolving Old Rehabilitation Issues

The gross insensitivity found in the sea bird project deeply exhorted us. We then decided to look into the issues pertaining to other projects like Adra, Karsalli and Kali projects. There too were some issues of rehabilitation. Many demands of the displaced people were not met. Some people had not received the alternate plots. So, I reviewed all those cases thoroughly. Wherever any discrepancy was found at any level, we made all efforts to see that even the individual grievances got redressed. In rehabilitation colonies also, we gave lots of grants from Zilla Parishad and other departments for development.

Development of Beach

We took many steps to promote tourism too. There

was a Fort by the side of Kali River. We developed that by creating wayside facilities. The historic Fort was basically the boundary of Maratha rule. Down below we had the resort. Another major work was development of the Coast—the beach of Karwar, which was very dirty. We took up a thorough cleaning drive for it. Since Mangalore's Pilikula project was in my mind, I thought a similar project for this area too. We found land near the beach where we planned a toy train around the beach area. We also built a musical fountain and planetarium. A small fish aquarium was there. We renovated that. It proved to be a big hit. Lot of plantation was done. We also wanted to make a swimming pool, because there are many swimmers from Karwar who compete at national level. But we could not do that due to some reasons.

Instructions to Avoid Anonymous Complaints

We also settled the issues pertaining to Konkan Railway. Some forest related issues like encroachment on forest land, smuggling of forest products, illegal cutting of the woods, etc. were also there. There were complaints that people coming from neighbouring states like Kerala settled in the interior areas and were involved in cutting of trees. Another interesting thing about Karwar was that (and it is recorded in the Gazette since the British period) you should not believe in anonymous complaints. I could see myself that 50% of the complaints were anonymous involving individual issues. The people had the habit of writing personal matters also to the administration.

Selling the Unsold

Since many people in Karwar are involved in jewellery work, we planned some projects for them also, but we could not execute them. I feel the district has not been developed as it should have been. It is close to Goa. It has a port, sea bird project, beaches, lots of rivers for river rafting, hydro power projects, backwaters, etc. but it was not developed accordingly. Kerala and Goa are now over-sold. Between them we have the best of the beaches in Karwar. But they are not as popular as they should have been. Om Beach is there. Lots of foreigners come, but many of them are not the kind of the tourists we want.

We also started literacy campaign on large scale involving the local people like the Siddis and others. Whatever experience we gained in Shimoga and Mangalore, we tried to replicate here. It was a wonderful experience. The composition of people in Karwar is different from other cities. Lethargy is very much there. But they are very much active for making complaints. Staff was OK, but majority of the posts were vacant, because the people were not interested in going there.

Wrote the Book 'Life and Peace'

As a whole, Karwar experience was enriching and relaxing. It was the place where I wrote my book, *'Life and Peace'*. I was somehow able to spare time to pen down certain experiences. I was there for about a year. Then I got permission to go for higher studies—masters in rural development—from the University of East Anglia in England. However, after doing my masters, I did not get work in rural development department. It happens with many people. What I experienced in the University was that 90% of their research was about Asian and African regions and it did not offer any concrete solution to those problems. □

Changing the Mindset

Additional Secretary, Department of Women and Child Development from September 11, 1998 to September 14, 1998

The Department of Women and Child Development, separated from Social Welfare Department in 1994, is responsible for the welfare and development of women, children, elderly and differently-abled. Besides implementing developmental programmes, it formulates necessary policies, programmes and schemes and also coordinates the efforts of both governmental and non-governmental organisations working for the upliftment of women, children, elderly and the differently-abled. Anganwadi workers also come under this department.

I went to the Department as Additional Secretary in 1998. The activities of the Department are known to me right from my first posting. Starting as Assistant Commissioner, then in Zilla Parishad and then as Deputy Commissioner, I was always in contact with the activities related to women and child welfare. Hence, I was aware of the problems of the Department and also of its potential. That is why I always wanted to work in this department for a longer duration for actual empowerment of the women.

Transformation in Social Mindset

The empowerment of women is indeed a challenge

for any society. Half of our population is women. Hence, unless they are empowered, real development of the country cannot take place. Their literacy rate is still low. Lots of health issues are there and they don't get priority in household affairs. The treatment meted out to the girl child is sometimes highly discriminatory. The Central and State governments are conducting lots of campaigns to generate awareness about girl child. Even then the issues are there in our Indian society. They get headlines in media at times. I wanted to work in this department.

When we were in the field, we used to hear about several incidents of exploitation of women. We also received complaints of exploitation of women staff by powerful groups and interests in the villages, exploitation by staff also in some cases especially by the supervisors. I wanted to tackle all these issues in this Department. However, I did not get that much time, but the issues were very sensitive and pertinent. This is the area where the real service can be done to a large section of the society. The foundation of a child going to Anganwadi centre is laid there. If we have the dedicated staff and supervisors, lots of changes can be brought about in the society. That is what I saw and still feel.

Exploitation of Devdasis

One has to deal in this department with the lots of important issues related to individuals and the society. A significant social problem in Karnataka is of Devdasis. In government, it is dealt by Women and Child Welfare Department. Once you study the issue deeply, you come to know about the pathetic situation. All the girls dedicated to the God in the name of Devdasis are mostly from one SC community in some parts of North Karnataka. They are basically poor people and the society has made the system such that the powerful people want to exploit them. So, they are dedicated in the name of God and are sexually exploited. The Department wanted to curb this bad practice and also uplift them. However, it has not happened so far. Many schemes have been launched and many benefits have been offered for them, but not much improvement has taken place. It is not that the people of other communities induce them in this activity; rather their own parents are involved in this social evil. That is how this social malady has continued. But it needs to be curbed at any cost.

In the Indian system, the preference for male child is still very much there. The lady of the house also prefers that only. If a young couple gets a female child, they do not celebrate, but if a male child is born they do. They think the posterity can be continued with male child only. The preference for male child results in discrimination with the girl child. This is seen in many parts of the country. It has to be fought by this Department. It is a big challenge for the Government and the Department. We have to bring changes in the society.

Blind Aping of the West is Dangerous

I had so many plans in my mind to execute in this Department, but could not because of the shortage of time. My posting in the Department was only for a few days. After some time I went to UK for higher studies—Masters in Rural Development. UK is a progressive society. Hence, the condition of women is much better there. They are equal in every sense of the term. Economic independence is there. In every walk of life, they are moving forward. That society is different and our society is different. You can see the contrast. Everybody who is in workable age gets work anywhere one wants. Education is also almost free there. Good quality education is imparted even in municipal schools. I spent good time there. I could know what difference in values we have. They want to enjoy the present. They are not much bothered about the past and the future. We should learn good values from them. But we have mostly adopted their outdated and rejected practices. Everything in the West is not good. We are far better than the West in many ways. Hence, instead of blindly aping them, we should be proud of our own values.

□

Enjoying Student Life After 22 Years

Masters in Rural Development from the University of East Anglia, Norwich, England, from September 1998 to September 1999

From Karwar, I was posted to the Department of Women and Child Development in 1998 for a brief period of four days. Then I went to the University of East Anglia in England to undergo Masters in Rural Development in September 1998. I have seen rural settings since my childhood and hence rural development has been very close to my heart. I wanted to know what is taught in that University to boost rural development activities. During that period in the University, I shared experiences with students from various countries. The faculty members showed lots of case studies on rural development during classes. The maximum case studies pertained to either Asian or African regions. There were no studies from any developed country. It may be because the concept of rural development is not there in that sense as is thought and practised in the developing countries.

What is in Classroom, is not on the Ground

Since I had extensively worked in the rural settings of Belgaum and Shimoga as Deputy Commissioner and also implemented various rural development schemes in

Mangalore and Karwar, I had practical experience in this sector. When I related those experiences with what we were taught in the classroom, I found what they were teaching had very limited impact. There was no concrete suggestion to overcome the problems faced by Indian villages. Our main concerns are poverty alleviation and taking the benefits of rural development schemes to the real beneficiaries. There is no dearth of resources. The problem is distribution—the delivery mechanism, identification of beneficiaries, transparency in delivery, etc. Those were the questions for which I was looking for answers, but, I did not get much of those. Anyway, we had to complete the study.

More than the study, the other part was also interesting. We could travel to other cities. I went to Paris along with the family. We saw Disneyland near Paris. We went to France by ship. For one cricket match, I went to another town to watch the Indian team playing against England. There were some extra-curricular activities too. I learnt how people did other things. We used to see our landlord, who himself repaired if any fault was occurred in the house. He had all the tools with him to repair the water tap, etc. It surprised us to see the old man doing all those works like plumbing, etc.

Noble Workmanship

The other interesting thing that we noticed in the urban areas of England was repairing of roads. One person comes with a vehicle, cut or open the place where the fault is, repairs the fault, packs it again and repairs the road and leaves. He does it in a single day. Such workmanship is unthinkable in our country. Here, normally a group of persons come to dig the road, and then they leave. After a few days, the next group comes to do the civil work. The group does some work, but does not fill it up. Then next agency comes to fill it up after several days and then next agency comes to repair the road. It takes months and months together to have coordination among various agencies.

Once the road is repaired, the next person again comes to dig it open for some other work. There is no coordination between the agencies.

Quality Services

In spite of all these settings and even working in various organisations, what I saw in England was very impressive. There are hilly areas. Even then the water pressure in the pipes is the same. It does not matter whether you stay at first floor, second floor or the third floor. On the other hand, what is seen in our country is that if the person on the ground or the first floor opens the tap, there is no water for the people on the top floors of the same building. These are the things that we learnt there.

Wife Worked in a Factory

My wife is not highly educated. But she also experienced working in some factories. When she went to the factory, I used to spend more time with the children. I dropped the children to school and then picked them up when the school was over. It was a fun and different type of life. I spent maximum time with the family and friends. We had four or five families in that building. We had good time as a family and as a group. In University too, we learnt a lot while interacting with the students, talking to them and sharing experiences. It was like living student life once again. Infrastructure facilities in the University were good. It was the year 1999-2000. Almost after 22 years, I enjoyed college life.

But whatever I learnt there, subsequently I did not get the opportunity to utilise that. It happens in governments. You are trained for something, but not always is the training made use of in postings. Sometimes they use the acquired knowledge, but mostly it is not considered while deciding the postings.

□

Difference in Learning in India and UK

Going to the University of East Anglia in Norwich, England, for higher studies was a good experience. I was already armed with the understanding of Indian education system from primary to University levels. It provided me the opportunity to understand the education system there. I could understand the school education system there because my own children studied there. I experienced the University system, because I myself did masters in Rural Development from the University of East Anglia. So, I saw how the schools functioned there, how the teachers got involved and what they taught in the class.

Stress-free Learning

The system there does not put much stress on a child at primary and secondary level. Hence, there is no question of carrying a bag full of textbooks and notebooks, what most students in India are seen carrying every day. The students leave their books in the school and come back home stress free. The stress of homework too is not there. When we met the students and teachers, we found their involvement was much more. They really spent time together and the teachers got involved with every child. Their dedication was much more than we see in most Indian schools. They continued to give new examples until the child learnt and understood the concept properly and they made them understand and cleared their doubts. They encouraged the students to ask more and more questions. That type of dedication I saw there.

Focus on Innovation and Creativity

The University system, which I experienced during my study of Rural Development, there is also different compared to the system prevailing in India. It is not a classroom in that sense. When the faculty members take classes, they narrate their first hand experiences and share the project reports. The homework that they normally give is also in the form of references. Hence, the students have to visit the library to search those references and finish the assignments. More emphasis is on preparing the student and helping him/her gain the knowledge. The student has to search the library, get references, understand the concept and then explain them in the class. Every student makes efforts. This way, the students spend more time in libraries, group discussions and making projects. When they work on projects, they become innovative, creative, analyse things, put the information in perspective and go through case studies. This makes them different in teaching the subjects.

India Follows Mostly Rejected Practices

On the other hand, the system followed in our country is chalk and talk. In most cases the teachers talk in the class and it is like a monologue. They keep talking on the subject. How much the students have understood its practical aspects, how are projects prepared, are not well integrated, as is done in the western countries. There, we used to participate in group discussions and play different roles in plays, games, etc. In that way, both learning systems are quite different. However, our ancient system of education in Gurukuls was like that only. But now they have adopted our ancient system and we have copied what they have rejected. Ours being such a vast country, we have lot to improve in our education system.

Difference in Lifestyle

The other thing that I noticed was the difference in the life in colonies and households. Here in India, we go and make friends and normally go to somebody's house. But nobody goes uninvited to somebody's house there. When somebody is invited, that person has to carry the drinks or whatever the host likes. Then they have dinner and spend time together. The life there is quite mechanical, which is not here in India. Here life is very lively. We have joint family system, respect for elders, normally three-four generations staying together. But, that is not there. Once the children are adult, they virtually throw them out to find their own ways. They go, find some partner, spend time together, take up a job and then start their life. Meeting their parents, etc. happens only on occasions or festivals.

Meticulous Methods of Attending Public Complaints

The thing that impressed me a lot was the manner in which they attended complaints and carried out public works. If we saw any leakage or fault on a road, somebody came driving the vehicle on his own, carrying all the required equipments in the shortest time possible. They cut the road, repair the fault and finish the work as if nothing happened. They attend to those things meticulously. I learnt those good values during my stay there. When you go to the market, you find everything organised. That culture has now captured Indian markets too, in the form of malls or foreign retail store chains.

Learning How to Go Digital

In those days, we learnt sending emails and using

computers. Prior to that, those things were not known much. I learnt how technology can be used in different ways. It helped me in the subsequent assignments in BESCOM, higher education department, etc. I emphasised on the use of technology to bring about more accountability and transparency in the system. That is why all the agencies and the governments are today stressing on adoption of technology. We are even entering in the cashless era. The change in the technology is so fast that what will happen tomorrow is difficult to predict today.

□

CHALLENGE OF 100% LITERACY

Many experiments have been conducted in the country since Independence in the form of schemes or programmes to ensure 100% literacy, but we are still far away from achieving the target. Sarva Shiksha Abhiyan and Right to Education have ensured good enrolment in schools but on the adult literacy front, the output is still not encouraging. National Literacy Mission (NLM) launched in 1988 to impart functional literacy to non-literates in the age group of 15-35 years in a time bound manner claimed to make 127.45 million people literates by the end of 10th Five Year Plan period. Similarly, Saakshar Bharat campaign was launched during the 11th Five Year Plan with the objective of raising literacy rate to 80% and reducing gender gap to 10%.

As per Census 2011, literacy rate in India stands at 72.98%. Overall Literacy rate grew by 8.14% points in the last decade (64.84% in 2001 & 72.98% in 2011). The states with literacy rate between national average (72.99%) and below 90% are Tripura (87.22%), Goa (88.70%), Daman & Diu (87.10%), Puducherry (85.85%), Chandigarh (86.05%), Delhi (86.21%), A&N Islands (86.63%), Himachal Pradesh (82.80%), Maharashtra (82.34%), Sikkim (81.42%) Tamil Nadu (80.09%), Nagaland (79.55%), Manipur (76.94%), Uttarakhand (78.82%), Gujarat (78.03%), Dadra & Nagar Haveli (76.24%), West Bengal (76.26%), Punjab (75.84%), Haryana (75.55%), Karnataka (75.36%) and Meghalaya (74.43%). Literacy rate in rural areas stands at 67.67% with rural male literacy rate 77.15% and rural female literacy rate 57.93%. Whereas literacy rate in urban areas stands at 84.11% with urban male literacy rate at 88.76% and urban female literacy at 79.11%. It requires the genuine involvement of the society to meet the challenge of 100% literacy.

Social Transformation sans Money

Director, Mass Education from September 1999 to December 1999

After returning from UK, I joined as Director, Mass Education in 1999. The tasks that I performed as Deputy Commissioner or CEO in various departments made me familiar with the schemes of both the Central and State Governments. The Total Literacy campaign in those days had turned into a mass movement. Lot of awareness was generated through various activities. The literacy campaign had been continuing for long, but I decided to make it sustainable, durable and more organised so that we achieve more positive results.

Creating a Chain of Dedicated Volunteers

The Total Literacy Campaign that I supervised in Belgaum and Shimoga brought me closer to the volunteers engaged in it. There were thousands of volunteers in each District. The volunteers were genuine people and were committed to the cause. They did everything possible to make the programme a big hit. Some of the examples were very encouraging, interesting and touching.

Starting from District Secretary of the Campaign down to the last volunteer, a chain was created—the chain of selfless volunteers. So, we knew the problems they faced, particularly the non-cooperation from the parties with vested interests, indifference of the people, ridiculous comments by some, etc. During this tenure, I wanted to support them and create a system wherein their continuity remained undisturbed and they are a part of the development process. We cannot expect everybody to always work selflessly. Every person has to look after their welfare too. That cannot be ignored. The voluntary work cannot be done at that cost. So, we wanted to integrate those volunteers in various schemes of the government depending on their eligibility. The objective was that they should not ignore their personal well-being.

Training the Volunteers

During that period, we trained and advised them to take advantage of the government schemes. We told the officers also that whatever they could pass should be passed. Not that they wanted or expected, but as emissaries to the government, we should respond to the people who do real social service. We brought those changes in the attitude of the Department personnel. We arranged several workshops and started working on those lines. During that period, I travelled to all districts of the state, went with the teams, interacted with the people, volunteers, NGOs and officers and motivated them. The whole atmosphere was recharged. The volunteers were very hopeful that we will do something substantial. Workshops were organised in Districts and Talukas. Even at block level, we started discussion with the Block Officers and Executive Officers.

Extraordinary Enthusiasm among Volunteers

During those interactions, we interacted with a large number of volunteers, including female volunteers and neo-literates. Their stories were interesting and they were successful in their areas. Many of them became members of Gram Panchayats, chairpersons, Taluk Panchayat members and even Zilla Parishad members. That type of empowerment developed in them. It was really fascinating to see such stories. In Mangalore, an 80 year old person who was a drunkard, abandoned drinking and started attending each and every function organised anywhere in the district or the state. His speech and experience inspired many people. There were many women who changed the habit of their husbands who used to drink. They became emboldened. Neo-literate clubs were also formed. Some of them started producing locally made products. Today, we see in Mangalore, the neo literates' experience is very good and they are very well-organised. A wave was created throughout the state in this way.

'Each One Teach Ten'

My tenure was limited as I had to go to the Government of India for my next assignment. But the experience of literacy campaign was indeed wonderful for me also. Practically, when we ask somebody to do voluntary work, the immediate response anybody gives would be that nothing can be done without money. But we educated them about what could be done without money. After interactions, the people themselves started suggesting a number of works, which did not require money. Total literacy is the issue in which a person can teach ten people—each one teach ten or each one teach one. Even plantation is possible without money. Inculcating a saving habit is also one.

Exceptional Hike in School Enrolment

The total literacy campaign was not only for making one literate or making him/her know how to put their signature. It was much more than that. The awareness among neo-literates about the importance of education was the most important thing. Most parents, without exception were further motivated to teach or send their children to schools. Enrollment increased in schools. No parent would say his child should remain an illiterate. They thought that it is enough that they are illiterate, but their children should never remain so. They worked hard or borrowed money to teach their children. That brought a lot of change in thinking process of the people.

The greatest contributions were giving up the bad habits, coming together for social causes, plantation, awareness for family planning, awareness for social forestry, doing *shramdan*, donation of books, collection of old toys, recirculation of old newspapers, book clubs, collection of plastic, making plastic-free villages, model villages, etc.

When we started talking, the people started believing and began joining hands in good numbers. The idea of doing work without money looked impractical in the beginning, but when we actually explained it, everybody accepted. That was the advantage of the Scheme.

□

A Dive in the Ocean of Governance

Director, Union Ministry of Steel, New Delhi from December 1999 to June 2001

The posting on central deputation in Union Ministry of Steel as Deputy Secretary in 1999 was enlightening in many senses. Before going there, I was posted in all the Districts of Karnataka and also finished higher studies in UK. But the atmosphere I found in the Central Secretariat in New Delhi was entirely different from the Secretariat in Bangalore—a very small cabin, unpunctual and inefficient staff. They always came late. They even disappeared any time for small pretexts like tea, coffee, etc.

Different Work Culture

Of course, we did not have many visitors there, because the timings for visitors were strict and no unwanted visitor was allowed to enter the Secretariat by the security personnel. The main file work happens at the Deputy Secretary and Joint Secretary levels, but the Under Secretary and down below Section Officers were not available most of the time. It was very difficult to get work done by them. The file arrangement was also different—note sheets were kept separate and the main correspondence file was kept separate. In Karnataka, we keep both together. My task was to deal with the PSUs. There were other Deputy Secretaries too, from different states and services. We met during lunch hour and shared our experiences. Other thing that they do in Government of India is that they don't affix the Service name after the designation and name. One does not know who belongs to which Service—the Indian Administrative Service or any other Service. It was good. It helps in intermixing of the officers.

Anarchist Traffic Arrangement

The Officers of Deputy Secretary level were not provided with transport facility. One had to make one's own arrangement. Hence, for the first time I bought a vehicle, a Maruti 800 car, on loan. I used to drive the car myself. First, I dropped my children to the school in the morning, and then came back home, got ready and reached office on time. That was the daily routine. Driving was definitely a challenge there, because the way some people used to drive was suicidal. You may drive carefully, but who might hit you when and where is not known. Until their vehicle come bumper to bumper they do not stop. People are very aggressive. We read about a lot of road rage incidents in newspapers almost every day. In some cases, people went on shooting others even on pity pretexts. If somebody does not give them side, they could go to any extent. There was a kind of anarchy on the roads. However, New Delhi area was better compare to the old Delhi. I lived in a two-bedroom quarter at Laxmibai Nagar. I spent more time with my family, as I did not have any other habit. On weekends or fortnight, I normally drove to my village in Rajasthan with the family. It was a five-day working in the Secretariat and I got plenty of time for myself there.

Good System of File Maintenance

The file maintenance system in Central Secretariat was good. They maintained old records, especially when the matter pertaining to questions in the Parliament. They had references of at least previous five years—what was the question and what was the reply so that they could relate both the questions and answers. They collected information pertaining to the questions from all over the country. That gives you the perspective of the whole country. While dealing in New Delhi, you have to see the equity too. In distribution of resources, however, there is no written instruction for allocation; still they give equal priority to all the states. It is not that anybody can corner the entire budget. They definitely maintain a balance. The system and procedure were better in the Secretariat. Then, the interference by People's Representatives i.e. MPs too was almost negligible at our level. They normally talked to the Secretaries or Joint Secretaries.

However, I did not like a few things. I was promoted to super time scale. Then one has the option to either stay in Delhi or go back to their respective state. There were some financial advantages too. But, I preferred coming back to Karnataka after a year and a half.

Need to Share the Best Practices

There is huge difference in the working at the Centre and the State. When you take a decision at the Centre, you are not sure whether it will be implemented or not. It goes to the states and somebody there implements that. So, there is no connection between the person taking the decision, implementing it or reviewing it. In State functioning, it is not like that. Here you can visualise the things, take a decision, send the decision down below and see whether it is being followed or not. This connect is here, which is missing at the Centre.

The interference in states is much more. People know that decision has been taken, they start asking about the implementation. Sometimes, they also try to influence the decision making. Then Minister also calls for feedback.

There is connection between what you have decided and what you are implementing. At the same time, you are not immune or insulated from the pulls and pressures, which are there in the Government of India. Much importance is accorded to the old files at the Centre, which is not so in the state where old files are mostly untraceable. The computerisation is less in state compared to the Centre. By and large, the system in both the states and the Centre has its own positives and negatives. There is a need to take the best of the practices from both the systems. The States can adopt good systems from the Centre, while the Centre can adopt good practices from the States.

Personal Experience

On personal front, of course, we had good time. Centre is the place where you can do lot of networking. If you want, you can develop contacts with the ministers, politicians, people in power, senior bureaucrats and the national press. However, Bangalore in that way, is better than other states because it is a big city. But in smaller states, you hardly see any activity. In terms of administration, the working in New Delhi was a good exposure for me. But nobody in the family was happy with the life in Delhi. Children used to ask whether we would stay in Delhi or go back to Bangalore. Finally, we returned and joined the state government.

In state, Director is the Head of the Department, but at the Centre it is not so. Between Joint Secretary and Under Secretary, there is a post of Director. They call it Deputy Secretary. Some officers who have completed particular assignments are called Directors. In Delhi, a Director is part of the Secretariat only. The connectivity with the people is more in the state, while at the Centre it is negligible. The vastness of the Government of India is so much that one gets lost. It is like an ocean. Diving in that ocean was indeed both interesting and educating.

□

Quality Construction without Middlemen

Managing Director, Karnataka Land Army Corporation, from June to July 2001

My posting in Karnataka Land Army Corporation as Managing Director in 2001 was for a brief duration—from June 16, 2001 to July 27, 2001—but it was an interesting phase in the Department. Started as a Directorate of Land Army in 1971 under the Rural Development Department of Government of Karnataka, it was incorporated as a Company in 1974 as Karnataka Land Army Corporation. It was renamed as Karnataka Rural Infrastructure Development Limited (KRIDL) in August 2008. It is a unique organisation of the Government of Karnataka involved in civil engineering construction and creation of assets in the state.

Employment to Rural People

KRIDL concentrates on labour intensive infrastructure works by providing employment opportunities to the rural unemployed and under-employed so as to improve their economic conditions. It undertakes rural development construction works directly by eliminating the middlemen i.e., contractors, to avoid exploitation of the rural poor, thereby passing on the full worth of money to the people.

Rejuvenating the Department

When I was posted in the Department, the Karnataka Transparency in Public Procurement (KTPP) Act was promulgated. Earlier, whatever tenders government department used to issue, they would get direct entrustment from the Department. But after the implementation of the Act, every Department was to adopt the tender route. No Department could give work to anybody unless the organisation is exempted. The exemption was also for a brief period of one year or so. Soon after taking over the Department, I discussed with the engineers the challenges before the Corporation and how to rejuvenate it and make sustainable for long term. I wanted the Department should not remain dependent on the government works only.

History of the Land Army Corporation is very interesting. The very name suggests that it has to do with army and the land. But in fact it has nothing to do with land development or the army. It was supposed to be people's army like providing jobs to people, ex-servicemen, others and avoid contracting in whatever works are given. Small works were taken up like construction of school or Anganwadi building, Janata houses, etc. Those works were entrusted directly to this department. This agency was not supposed to call tenders as it was not a contracting agency. It was supposed to do work directly by engaging the public, procuring the material and finishing the work at the cheapest cost. Providing employment to the rural people was also one of the objectives. It was started with good intentions. However, now it has become like a contract agency doing the civil construction work of various departments. Finance Department gives it exemption from time to time. According to that exemption, they get works from various departments.

Motivation for Pan India Presence

When I joined the Department, we did a lot of

brainstorming with the engineers as to how the land army can be diversified. We even declared incentives for the engineers who bring civil construction work from private parties. With that concept, we started thinking of reforms. We also motivated them to do private consultancy. If somebody wants consultancy or guidance for construction of houses, design, architecture, etc, the agency should provide those things too. Normally, the private consultants charge more, but we could charge less. We prepared the engineers like that.

The KRIDL was operating in Karnataka alone. We motivated it to participate in the tenders anywhere in the country like Uttar Pradesh Bridge Construction Corporation participates everywhere. They were quite enthusiastic. The activities began and the turnover within two months suddenly jumped. All people working in the Department geared up to take up new challenges. Of course, after my transfer to the Housing Board, not much happened and they continued the same work. The concept of Land Army is actually very good—eliminating the middlemen and doing the work at cheap rates.

Quality Construction – Sole Objective

The common complaint against the Land Army was the poor quality of construction. That was a challenge and that image had to be changed. Wherever the officer is good down below, the quality of work is good. If there is supervision from the interested agency then also the quality is good. If there is no supervision and the officer too is not good, poor quality work takes place. The challenge before us was to change this image and ensure that there would be good quality work even if there is no supervision. It is must to enhance the image of the Corporation. In the absence of proper supervision, the building may look attractive from outside, but during rainy season it may leak or internally the building may not be strong. Wood work may also be poor. Most of the complaints against the Corporation were of that nature.

Need to Popularise the Concept

Despite some complaints, good work is done by the Department. In fact, there is no parallel to it even in Delhi. National Building Construction Corporation (NBCC) and many other big organisations are there, but they undertake big contracts only. There is lot of difference in their working and KRIDL's working. KRIDL does not take the big works, but small assignments only. The reputation of the Land Army basically depends upon the officers. If officers are good, good quality work will take place and the reputation will be good. If the officers are bad, the whole organisation is blamed.

I feel there is huge scope for popularising the basic concept of KRIDL. At times, when contractors fleece the governments and the system, such organisations, if function efficiently, can offer good solution to many problems.

□

Affordable Housing Indeed

Housing Commissioner, Karnataka Housing Board, from July 2001 to March 2003

From Karnataka Land Army Corporation, I was posted to Karnataka Housing Board (KHB) as Housing Commissioner in 2001, which was then in a very poor financial condition. Rather, it was on the verge of closure. There were serious discussions in some circles to shut it down, because it had lost its utility and reached a stage where it was believed to be difficult to revive. At that point of time, my predecessor, who later became Chief Secretary, planned '100 Housing' project at majority of the locations.

Pushing '100 Housing' Project

The Board had properties at more than 100 locations, but had no concrete plan for their development. To make the best use of those properties, he pushed the '100 Housing' project. When I came here, it was only at the concept stage. I decided to further push it. Hence, we empanelled architects and made them Project Monitoring Consultants (PMCs). We assigned them work on Turnkey basis—Turn key without variation. There was no variation clause. The tender value was final. I monitored the project on a weekly basis. Since the beginning, it was put on fast track. Soon it started taking a shape. Since we had empanelled the best of the architects, the design of the houses was out of the box—eco-friendly and energy-efficient.

The major challenge before us in the Housing Board was its poor reputation. That is why it had lot of unsold stock of houses. One of the unsold stocks was, apart from the National Housing Game Project, at Yalahanka Satellite Township. Most of the houses of certain categories were vacant in many areas. Poor quality was the main complaint. People came to buy a Housing Board house only for title, because the land title was clear, and not for the quality construction. We engaged an agency, pushed advertising drive and started clearing the old stock not only in Yalahanka (Bangalore), but also in other district headquarters like Hasan. We started giving houses on first come first serve basis. Whosoever applied was given the house. That is how we could liquidate both the stock of houses and the loan on the Housing Board.

Joining Hands with Private Parties

The other area planned by the Housing Board was joint development involving other parties including the private parties. Even sharing the name of the Housing Board with promoters was discussed. We had open mind. In those days, the Housing Board reputation improved due to the construction of good quality houses. In certain areas like Bidar, Mandya, Mysore and Mangalore, the demand became so high that we did not even have enough land. At some places, the people had left the land, which was encroached upon by some people. We removed that encroachment.

Resolving Old Disputes

There were a large number of old cases like title disputes or individual petitions, which were not settled. I heard them on a weekly basis. Of course, as usual, wherever I go I don't hold back the people and see them whenever they come. We had lots of connections with HUDCC. It was willing to support us in a big way. The Housing Board gradually acquired good reputation and expertise because of the good architects that we had hired.

Another initiative, which I took and which later proved to be a milestone, was taking work from other departments. For example, I approached the then Revenue Minister. Then seven new districts had been carved out and they needed District Office Complexes. Initially, we could take the work of five districts, except Udupi and Gadag. We made good architectural plans for those office complexes, and got the building design prepared by the nationally reputed architects. After the Deputy Commissioner's feedback, we were awarded the tenders of those works. Later on, the work of the other two districts was also assigned to us. By and large all seven office complexes were built by the Housing Board. They were marvellous. With the construction of those buildings, the reputation of the Board further improved.

Turning the Tide

Then the '100 Housing' scheme, was under implementation and the houses were coming up in time, the people started displaying enthusiastic response when we invited applications. The quality of the houses was a surprise for everyone. Once we allotted the houses, the allottees knew which house they had been allotted. So, they also monitored the work while it was under construction. They could see the work, do any value addition or even suggest changes. That too we allowed. If somebody wanted that kitchen should not be here and the bedroom should be in that direction or some other small changes, those too were allowed. Because the person who has to live there should be happy with the house. We went to that extent accommodating the views of the prospective buyers so that after completion they do not require any major modifications.

Progressive Decision-Making

That was a big change in our thinking. Whatever variation in the modification was there that was factored. If it required costly material, that was charged and if there was not much change, it was not. That was hugely welcomed by the people. When people came to know about this major shift in the thinking, many unsold houses were also purchased by the people. They thank us even today. We could recover the dues from the public and we liquidated our liability towards the HUDCO and other organisations. We also restructured the loan, because high interest loans were taken from many institutions. We negotiated with the HUDCO and the banks. We gave our deposits to whichever bank offered lesser interest rates. We could save lot of money on that count for the Housing Board. In those days, a kind of progressive thinking was there in the management and decision making. One more interesting thing was that the public grievances were settled swiftly. Some rental housing schemes were also there.

A house is very dear to everyone. That is why the percentage of defaulters was very low. That was another interesting thing. They paid the installments in time even if they had to economise elsewhere. In slum areas too, we took up developmental work. Slum Clearance Board houses were there and the Housing Board helped them too. By and large, it was an enriching experience for me.

□

The Trade Union Leader Who Changed My Approach

Managing Director, BESCOM from March 2003 to July 2005

From Housing Board, I was moved to Bangalore Electric Supply Company Ltd. (BESCOM) as Managing Director in 2003. It is one of the five electricity supply companies carved out of the erstwhile Karnataka Electricity Board (KEB). Karnataka Power Transmission Corporation Limited (KPTCL) became the transmission company and the BESCOM as well as other companies became supply companies. My earlier experience of working in the KEB as Secretary was mostly about administrative matters. But in the BESCOM, I had to look after the technical affairs also. Supply of the electricity at substation or consumer level was the main activity. However, it covered lots of activities.

Generating Revenue from the Invisible

It was quite interesting and a new subject for me to understand the total concept of electricity supply, revenue model, grievances of the people, etc. Electricity is the kind of thing, which is invisible. In Housing Board, you can see the houses or flats which have been built or the sites that have been allotted. But here you cannot see anything. You know only the consumers, who consume the thing and pay revenue. Therefore, the consumers pay revenue for the thing, which is measured, but is intangible.

Turning Losses into Profits

It was indeed a challenge for me to renovate the old infrastructure. The LT and HT lines were laid long ago. Renovating them was a major challenge, because the BESCOM was not in a good financial position. That is why talks of privatising electric supply in Bangalore were seriously going on. It was a challenge for me to make BESCOM financially viable. If a company cannot become financially viable in a city like Bangalore, then it cannot become viable anywhere else.

Reduction in transmission and distribution losses was the main challenge. Additionally, a large number of consumers came with grievances in various offices. How to solve their problems and how to make systemic changes was also a challenge. Many consumers came with the grievances that they have applied for connection, but are not being granted. Even industries were not being served on priority. Principally, the segment, which pays more revenue, should be served first. But, there were complaints that the transformers cannot bear the additional load. The system was already overloaded. Therefore, adding new consumers was not possible. There were challenges on every front.

Manual Billing – Zero Computerisation

There was zero computerisation at that time. Bills were generated manually. So, many complaints were there on that account only. The people dealing the billing section used to make pencil entries raising high bills. When the consumer came, they corrected it (may be after some considerations) and give it back to the consumers. Proper accounting was not being followed. That is why there was huge loss in terms of unit and revenue both. Such challenges were there before me.

Overall Upgradation of the System

Since BESCOM was a leading company in the state capital, I had to show the results. Quickly, I familiarised myself with the working. I started holding meetings with the engineers, talking to people, hearing the grievances of public. As usual, I did not have any visiting hours. Anybody could have come to me anytime with a complaint. I continued that practice here also. I started dialogue with the employees unions and discussed computerisation and other things. Then we needed to make lots of project plans for Accelerate Power Development Reforms Programme (APDRP), a Government of India funded scheme, under which we had to make lots of schemes for upgradation of the system. We got the scheme sanctioned, but its implementation was again a challenge with the same employees. There were diverse challenges—administrative, project implementation on time and taking people together.

As in the KEB, the employees were not bifurcated. The KEB employees were there but they were not assigned to SCOMs. In those days, the employees unions were very strong in terms of interference in administrative and other matters. Taking any radical decision was very difficult. If they started objecting, that became a problem. The challenge was to run the system efficiently, to plug the leakages in the system, implement the improvements and at the same time reduce the losses and increase the revenue and then orient the staff to behave properly with the public while addressing their grievances.

Informal Meetings

I introduced the concept of weekly meetings. Every week I met the main officers at head office and also the engineers working in the field. Normally, the people meet during the important meetings. But here we met every week. Meeting and talking to them informally was my way of doing things. I do not believe in exercising the official authority, I rather believe in using the personal authority. If you know somebody personally, you can get more work done from him. We have powers to use, we can penalise anyone. But that should be the last resort. That is what I believe. I orally threatened to take action, but I never took punitive action against the officers (like suspending them or taking disciplinary action). Terrorising the staff and then getting work done was not my style of functioning.

Issues with Employees' Union

I mention here an incident, which shows how we normally adjust our strategy. I passed orders for transferring a few people based on some complaints. The then employees' union general secretary, whom I knew for a long time, came to me. He told me to reconsider some of the transfer orders. I said, once I have passed the orders I would not change a single word. Then he went. Next day, he again came and said I want to talk to you, sir. I said "yes, tell me what the matter is". He again asked to at least modify the orders pertaining some people. I again declined his request. Then he said what do you want as MD—whether you want to just implement these orders or you want to do something good for the Company. I said I want to do something good for the Company. Then he said you don't stick to this order. Order is not important. Because as MD you will do so many good things if you stay here. If we agitate and you accelerate the issue, the insignificant issues will become main issues. If you are shifted somewhere else you will not be able to implement your ideas. I liked the way he put that thing. Then I realised there is no point in confrontation. If they cooperate on bigger issues, then the smaller issues become insignificant. So, I accommodated and made some changes in the order. They were very happy and in future they supported us.

Nothing Personal

I learnt from that union leader that we should not be adamant. It is better to accommodate the smaller things to gain bigger ones, which benefit the larger group of people. There is nothing personal. If X is working somewhere, if he works at Y place, it does not matter for the organisation. I remember what he said.

He was a very practical and pragmatic person. We used to negotiate on wages and other issues. The unions continue to fight for their demands, but an officer has to think many things before accepting any demand. But the genuine demands should be accepted without delay.

□

ARRESTING POWER PILFERAGE

As technology is entering every aspect of life, the demand for electricity is increasing unexpectedly. Everyone wants uninterrupted electric supply, but many do not think it is necessary to pay for it, which causes huge loss to the power agencies. Reports reveal that only half of the revenue is realised in the power sector. According to 'Emerging Markets Smart Grid: Outlook 2015', India witnesses highest power losses ($16.2 billion), followed by Brazil ($10.5 billion) and Russia ($5.1 billion). In states, Maharashtra alone loses $2.8 billion per year—more than all but eight countries in the world. Nationally, total transmission and distribution losses approach 23% and losses in some states exceeds 50%.

In November 2014, the Central Government declared to spend 253 billion rupees on tackling rampant electricity theft by rolling out metering in cities and upgrading the old distribution networks. The Centre estimated that about 40% of the electricity goes unpaid for in some states, especially where cheap or free power has been offered in greed of votes by some political parties. Now courts are also in favour of taking stern action against the power thieves. Bombay High Court on August 26, 2014 ordered setting up of a "special cell" comprising of chief vigilance officer of Brihanmumbai Electric Supply and Transport Undertaking (BEST) and Deputy Commissioner of Police (operations) to keep a check on power thefts. The country spends huge sums of money on power generation. If the people do not pay for the electricity they consume, how will the power companies survive? No government can afford it.

Loss-Making BESCOM Earns Huge Profit

Reform was the main thrust of my activities in Bangalore Electric Supply Company Ltd (BESCOM), which I had joined in 2003 as the Managing Director. The system of producing manual bills was not only a form of harassing the honest consumers, but also causing major loss to the Company. Till 2002, the bills were prepared and served to the consumers manually. As a solution, I decided to fully computerise the billing process. It was the first reform that I had in my mind even before joining the Company. As I started action on computerisation and on understanding the whole mechanism, I found that the TCS Company had done some work on computerisation, but it could not complete it due to some reasons. It was almost half done. Software was not ready. Therefore, preparing the software as per the changing needs was the immediate challenge ahead.

Computerisation of Billing Process

As the discussion about computerisation began, it received, as was expected, sharp reaction from the employees. We persuaded them by ensuring that their interests will be protected. Even then they insisted that they would continue to write ledgers manually. I allowed them and also paid them remuneration for it for some time. We simultaneously started preparing the software and modernisation by installing computers and training the staff for proper handling of the machines. Even after preparing the software and computerising the whole system, the employees were not convinced to depend upon it. Therefore, we allowed both the systems —manual and computerised—parallelly. That is how we started doing the things. It took about three-four months for the staff to fully get habitual of the new system. Then we started generating and serving computerised bills only. Then we procured some hand-held machines to further modernise the system. The hand-held machines helped the staff record the units manually and produce the bills for consumers instantly.

Energy Audit

Another major reform was energy audit. It is like a balance sheet showing how many units were received, how many were sold and how much revenue was generated. We took power from one source and supplied it to the consumers. In the process there are transmission losses and the revenue we received then is the balance. Energy audit was a major challenge for us. During the computerisation process, I suddenly thought of making energy auditing a part of the system. Normally, energy audit is done by an external agency. Their people come, assess the losses and then show the results. But it was not convincing. I thought of making it more practical especially after introducing the computers.

Mapping the Network

The idea that clicked in my mind for internal energy audit was mapping the entire network. We decided to record the energy units that we receive from generating station to our sub-station. A meter was put on the station from where the electricity is dispatched to the 11 KV feeders.

It recorded how much energy was dispatched. Distribution Transformers (DTs) are points up to which 11 KV power comes through high tension level. Then it is stepped down to Low Tension or LT level. From LT, it goes to the individual consumers. So, Transformer is the point where we decided to install the meter and measure the energy—how much energy has come to this level and how many consumers are connected to the transformer.

Earlier the meter reading was taken according to the whims and fancies of the meter readers. We decided to take the meter reading according to the map that we had decided. We mapped all the points—transformers, below transformers and the individual consumers. The meter readers then used to read about 300 to 400 meters in a day. We told them to read that number only, but read according to the map and do it on the same day. All meters coming under a transformer should be read on the same day. The meter installed at the transformer recorded the units it transmitted. Then, how many units were consumed by the consumers is also recorded. Then, we tally it with the total units supplied and minus the system losses.

This way we could map all the 10,000 transformers in Bangalore. Now by default we could know how much the losses were and where—10%, 20%, 30%, 50% or 100%. At some places, it was indeed 100% loss. We thought how is a 70 or 100% loss possible? First, we closely monitored the transformers, which recorded more than 20% loss. We started checking every installation by forming squads. That way the energy audit happened automatically every month—how much is received at the transformer level, how much is supplied to the consumers and what is the difference.

During the monitoring, we found that many houses had faulty meters, tampered meters or non-functional meters. We addressed them also, by changing the meters. To our surprise, not only the revenue increased substantially but also the public complaints became negligible. This also put a check on the informal understanding between the individuals and meter readers. We could also identify the high loss making areas. In four-five months, we streamlined the system and brought down loses to merely 9%. Earlier, the losses were 17%. It resulted in annual revenue generation of more than ₹ 500 crore—without doing anything. The formula, which worked was mapping the network on paper and working accordingly. Otherwise, there was no other way to check every meter every month.

The Bangalore Model

The Bangalore Model of curbing energy losses received attention of many states. Hence, it was adopted everywhere. In urban areas, it was a big hit. Through this method, we could detect the losses at each transformer level. Then we made the reading at Transformer, HT and LT level automatic. Meter readers did not require going there. They could do it through remote control any time. Then we also upgraded the system like repairing the technical faults, overcoming overloading, upgrading the LT lines to HT lines, etc. By and large, lots of reforms were introduced. During my tenure, the loss making BESCOM, which was to be closed down or privatised, was rated as the best profit making company. Then it started supporting the other SCOMs too.

This is how we ensured absolute consumer satisfaction and profit in the business. The tool that helped us in this endeavour was the use of the best available technology and adoption of the best practices in power sector. I believe that the goal should be to have customer service that is not just the best but legendry. Now the BESCOM is responsible for power distribution in eight districts—Bangalore Urban/ Rural, Kolar, Tumkur, Ramanagar, Chikkaballapura, Chitradurga and Davangere. It covers an area of 41,092 sq. km with a population of over 207 lakh. It serves about 93 lakh consumers today. The expansion in the network is because of the quality service that it tries to ensure each and every consumer. Unless you have 100 per cent customer satisfaction ...you must improve.

□

Grievance Redressal in BESCOM

In a public utility company, handling and reducing public grievances is a challenge for any Administrator. BESCOM, which I had joined in 2003 as the Managing Director, was no exception. Having Bangalore metropolitan city in its hold, it has very enlightened customers who have high expectations from it. They want to get best of the power supply. Many of them go abroad and compare the services available there. On the other hand, there are rural areas where too the people have permanent complaints regarding power supply and billing. During my tenure in the BESCOM, I focused on it right from the beginning.

While analysing I found that majority of the complaints, more than 80%, were about faulty billing. About 15% pertained to system faults and 5% were miscellaneous. Even after so many complaints the people faced difficulties in registering their grievances. As a first step, we immediately upgraded the Interactive Voice Response System (IVRS), deputed the staff to record grievances round the clock and also increased the number of telephone lines in the control room. Their duty was to hear, record and redress the grievances round the clock.

Phone-in Programme on All India Radio

Since the computerisation of billing system reduced the complaints substantially, we further strengthened the system. We checked how many complaints were there, monitored them on a weekly basis and then followed up.

The other major initiative that helped us reducing the grievances was introduction of phone-in programme on All India Radio. I requested the All India Radio to record the complaints of people 24 hours. A large number of people registered their complaints both in our office and also with the All India Radio. We launched the phone-in programme by taking some dedicated phone lines.

We invited the then CEO of Prasar Bharati Board to launch the programme. During our discussion, he jokingly said "why are you creating problem for yourself?" He said people would start directly calling you and everybody would expect redressal of the problem from you. I said "that is what we are meant for. Even if they call and stress us out, we will not mind and we will do that". He said, "OK, go ahead." This is how we introduced the phone-in programme. For that programme, I personally went to AIR office on a weekly basis. I also took officers along. We recorded all the call details—who called and what the grievance was. We also stored the recorded version, which was on the same day or the next day transcribed and emailed or faxed to the concerned officers. Within a week they had to give compliance. At that time we got 25 to 30 complaints per hour on phone. We compiled them. Over a period, the success rate of positive action went up to 90%. Later on, it improved to 95% also.

Winning Public Confidence

The phone-in programme generated a confidence among the public, assuring them that some action is surely taken on their complaints. People used to directly ask the officers what action had been taken on their complaint, if they did not receive compliance. After few months, the response to the phone-in programme was so much that hundreds of calls waited during every hour of the programme. Everybody wanted to talk to me for Redressal of the complaints. Through that programme we did not take individual complaints pertaining to service matters but only the individual complaints related to energy.

Increase in Accountability

The credibility of the programme was so much that people started calling the officers to take up their complaint; otherwise they would talk to the MD through phone-in programme. The officers also responded positively and did not dismiss the complaints. It also made the officers more responsive and accountable. I could not have introduced that much accountability through any other system. Anybody from the state could call me anytime. The officers also knew that any call can come from anywhere, and at anytime. Every officer was alert. People still remember that mechanism. If I go to AIR for any other programme, people still share their good experiences from that time.

In one case, an employee took bribe for some work. The complaint reached us through phone-in programme. It scared the employee so much that he personally visited the complainant, apologised, returned the money and said "please don't follow it up". He did it on his own. We did not say anything. While recording the complaint, we used to take only the gist and then the officer concerned used to call the person again to know his problem in detail. It all resulted in responsive administration, which was a major achievement.

Instant Reading – Instant Bill

The upgradation of IVR system—an automated telephony system that interacts with callers, gathers information and routes calls to the appropriate recipient also proved very helpful. After computerised billing, we introduced on-the-spot billing in which the meter reader did not require to take reading manually, come back to the office and again go back to deliver the bill. The hand-held machines that we provided to each meter reader generated bills immediately after recording the meter reading. So, we could give the bills to the consumers instantly and collect payment also if one wanted to pay. It became a very efficient way of handling the public grievances. Similarly, in rural areas we monitored the complaints of consumers.

Employees' Insurance

We also addressed the grievances and problems of our employees. In any electricity department, lineman is the person, who goes to the most dangerous area. We gave them kits for their safety. It reduced the number of fatalities. We also insured them up to ₹ 10 lakh for the eventuality if they meet any accident. It became a model for others too.

Round the Clock Payment Kiosks

Another initiative that we introduced was round the clock payment kiosks. Earlier, the payments could be received only between 10 am to 5 pm, which proved very inconvenient for the working persons. For the first time in the country, we thought of and implemented the 'anytime payment kiosks' where people could make payment through any mode—cheque, cash, DD, debit card, etc. The receipt was also given instantly. People, during morning walk or after having dinner at night could also pay their bills at the kiosks. That experiment proved to be a big hit. That too helped in reducing the grievances. The long queues, normally witnessed at payment collection centres during the day time, became a thing of the past. In the changing scenario as the complications in life are increasing, the Administration needs to make the things easier and convenient.

□

Promoting Judicious Irrigation

Managing Director, Cauvery Neeravari Nigam Ltd. from July 2005 to August 2005

After Bangalore Electricity Supply Company Limited (BESCOM), my posting was in the irrigation sector for direct experience. In the year 2005, I took over as the Managing Director of Cauvery Neeravari Nigam Ltd, which covers the projects coming under the Cauvery basin. The Nigam is basically a Corporation constituted to improve the irrigation projects in Cauvery basin area. Initially, I thought it is a very small project, but when I toured all the projects, I found it to be a huge organisation with a vast network. There was a huge potential of working there.

Awareness about Water Harvesting

First, I wanted to make a Master Plan for entire area and a plan for promoting the optimal use of water. I thought if I continued here for a longer period, I would ensure water harvesting everywhere—every inch of land receives water, water gets percolated in the land so that minimum water flows in the basin area and then remaining water goes to a reservoir. My plan was that all the areas—irrigation area, forest area and other areas—should get water harvesting structures. Consciousness about water was to be brought in the minds of the people so that maximum benefit is derived by them. I took it up on fast track basis.

Cost-Benefit Analysis

My second emphasis was the command areas—the areas with reservoirs and where the water was used for irrigation purpose. I wanted that the farmers should be aware of the importance of water. Just because a dam is constructed and water is stored there, they should not use water unscientifically. Only that much water should be used which is required by the crops. Instead of promoting water intensive crops, the focus was shifted to encourage the farming of the crops, which require lesser water. We also started discussing the cost benefit analysis with the farmers. Their general tendency was to grow paddy and sugarcane, which require lots of water. They found them easier to grow. But with that much water they could grow lots of horticultural crops in a big way.

The Fallacy of Lift Irrigation

I inspected all the irrigation projects, including those, which were yet to be completed. I found that my predecessors in the Department had planned several lift irrigation schemes. Many of those schemes were unviable. Massive projects were planned, electric sub stations were built spending huge sums of money, but the actual use of projects was minimal and many of them were not functional. Lot of power is consumed in pumping the water and irrigating the areas. It becomes an unviable thing. So, I decided to discourage more lift irrigation schemes, especially the bigger ones, which required huge expenditure on power bills.

Tourist Destinations near Dams

The other areas, which I identified for development, were the vast tracks of land lying vacant below most of the irrigation dams. Some parts of that land had been encroached. Even plantation was not done there. In Karnataka, we have a model of Krishna Raja Sagara (KRS) dam. Below the dam good gardens have been developed, which are now good tourist attractions. Such tourist attractions were planned with public participation under the dams. There are so many dams, which could have been developed on that pattern. It was possible at many places like Harangi dam, Gorur Dam, Gundlupet dam in Mysore, etc. Lot of wasteland was there down below the dams. We wanted to develop that on PPP model. We called tenders for it and some entrepreneurs too displayed keen interest in some of the projects.

Keeping all these thoughts in mind, we tried to prepare project reports. But the time at my disposal was limited. There is huge scope of showing the proper use of water, making people aware of the importance of water, conserving rainwater and using it optimally. That potential is still there in these areas. There was good scope of interacting with the farmers in this department. Since some of the farmers were growing tobacco, there was an emphasis on converting that land for other crops so that they contribute something constructive to the society through their farming.

Educating People on Water Consumption

Being a person from an agricultural background, it was close to my scheme of thinking. Coming from Rajasthan, I know the importance of water. In Rajasthan, what people do is that they draw water from the wells, where mostly women bring water, they don't take bathe daily but once in a few days. When they bathe, they sit on a cot, and below it they keep a big pot to store that water which would have gone wasted otherwise. With that water, they wash clothes. After washing the clothes they offer that water to animals for drinking. If any water is still left after the animals use, they water the plants. The same water has four uses in a day. That is the importance of water. Water is life. Nothing is possible without water. That importance has to be understood everywhere. Especially today, it is much more important.

Huge quantity of water is supplied to Bangalore from Cauvery. Over a hundred km pipeline has been laid from the River to the city. That shows the efforts put into supplying water. The importance of water is understood more by those who have faced scarcity of drinking water. The importance of water has to be told to everyone. If we fail to save water today, there may not be water for the future generations. Therefore, water conservation has to be done on large scale and every citizen has to contribute in it.

□

Revolutionising the Power Supply

Managing Director, KPTCL, from August 2005 to June 2008

As part of the extensive reforms in power sector, Karnataka Power Transmission Corporation Ltd. (KPTCL) was carved out as a transmission company after bifurcation of Karnataka Electricity Board (KEB). Its responsibility is to supply power from the generating stations to the substation level. It was in a very poor state when I took over as its Managing Director in August 2005. There were many challenges before us. As experienced at many places, the transformers and sub stations were heavily overloaded. They were not even in the position to supply power to HT consumers. Since prime source of revenue in this department are the HT consumers, supply to those consumers too was not a priority due to the poor network. In fact, I had experienced all these problems when I was in BESCOM. So, addressing them effectively was already in my mind.

Commissioning a New Station Every Day

Right from day one, we worked in mission mode. I told the officers to prepare an aggressive plan for creating new high capacity stations and upgrading the existing network. During initial review, I found that the officers were finishing from 20 to 25 stations annually. The number of stations undertaken was also not much. So, I conducted a complete review of the requirements at all locations, and where the stations were overloaded. We found the situation to be very grim. The network was not in a position to bear further load, but new consumers were being added continuously. So, the immediate task before us was to create more stations in order to save the entire network from a total collapse. I told the engineers to prepare plans on a war footing. I gave them a fancy target—to commission a new station every day after one year, hence creating 365 stations in a year. The engineers said it was impossible. They were not habitual of taking up such a big challenge. I motivated them to think high. So, they stood up with renewed vigour and formulated plans accordingly.

Synchronising Different Tasks

When reviewed why the execution of new stations was not happening speedily, we found, we were encountering various shortcomings. One of them was that many agencies were involved in the execution of one station. One agency created station, the second laid down lines, the third did other work and the fourth something else. It was not synchronised. Another problem was that the individual contractor, who was carrying out the station work, was himself placing orders for transformers, and the transformer suppliers were not giving them priority. At many stations, it was witnessed that everything was ready but the transformer was not available. Hence, the station could not be commissioned. At some places, land acquisition was a problem, while somewhere else the lines were getting delayed. So, then onwards we decided to give the whole work of a station to one contractor only—both station and the transmission line. Both have to be in sync.

Biggest Tender to Procure Transformers

That initiative eliminated a lots of problems. Since there was a delay in transformers' supply, we decided to procure transformers ourselves. We assessed the requirement for the next one year and invited separate tenders for supply of transformers. At that point of time, it was the biggest tender in the country for supply of transformers. Thus, wherever the stations came close to commissioning, we provided them with transformers and the delay was avoided. When the work of a station and line was given to the same contractor, that also eliminated delays to a great extent. I reviewed the progress on weekly basis. When I left office after two years, I was surprised to know that more than 250 stations had been commissioned. It eased the constraints and losses got reduced. The power losses, which were about 8% earlier, came down to 4%. It was because of the improvement in the system. It was done with the same staff members. They were motivated to take up work on fast track and instructions were issued to achieve the target within the time limit.

Interconnecting Power Stations

The other major thing that subsequently happened was interconnection of 400 KV stations, which were not connected earlier. Some 220 KV stations were also there. They were not interlinked in city areas. Hence, it was not possible to supply power from one area to the other in case of a power failure or any mishap. In a major initiative, we interconnected majority of them. In Bangalore, all 400, 220 or 66 KV stations are interconnected. If power fails at one source, we can restore power supply from the other source without delay. That type of networking was done by us through cables.

Creating Unmanned Stations

Another revolutionary step that we took in the KPTCL was introduction of Supervisory Control and Data Acquisition (SCADA) scheme. The scheme turned the entire power supply high-tech, reducing the manual interference. The dream of unmanned stations came true. Everything was available on the computer. Which distribution station has power and which does not was all available on the computer screen. We could even control overloading; or switch the power supply on or off in any area. We were able to manage the entire station technologically without any manpower. It is like remote monitoring. Bangalore was then the first city to have all stations automated using SCADA. We upgraded the technology to that extent.

All these efforts changed the picture of the KPTCL within two years. The company, which was at the verge of collapse, became a leader in the use of technology. We need to dream high and take steps accordingly to achieve extraordinary results.

□

Setting High Standards in Customer Care

If we could revolutionise the working of KPTCL, BESCOM or the SCOMs in Karnataka within a short duration, it was because of the collective efforts of the all staff members. Majority of the employees were earlier part of the Karnataka Electricity Board (KEB). Since beginning, I have been of the firm opinion that motivation and training to staff pay huge dividends. Therefore, while introducing new schemes in KPTCL or BESCOM, we paid equal attention to imparting requisite training to the employees. That training also included making them aware of their duties and responsibilities. Transparency and accountability too were a priority.

Full Proof Mechanism to Redress Grievances

We continued the phone-in-programme that we had started in BESCOM, in KPTCL too. The programme was a big hit to connect to the consumers. Whosoever had any grievance, he/she could have conveyed the matter to the authorities concerned and their grievances were heard and addressed to a satisfactory level. We also continued the best practices, being initiated and practised in the SCOMs, in the KPTCL also. The energy audit that we had started in the BESCOM was started in the SCOMs too. More emphasis was laid on grievance redressal—the public complaints had to be attended and a reply had to be given on the same day, and no complaint must remain pending for the next day. We made the employees accountable to that level for regaining and strengthening the trust of the consumers.

Phone-in Programme on 'Doordarshan'

The financial support that we received from the Government of India under Accelerated Power Development and Reforms Programme (APDRP) proved very helpful in introducing some new practices like grievance handling, system improvement, etc. We also recruited employees, as there was an acute shortage of employees at JE, AE and linemen levels. That was done very sincerely in the KPTCL and SCOMs. Because I was chairman of all the SCOMs also, for me controlling all the SCOMs was easy. If any good practice was there in one SCOM, that was transferred to the other SCOMs also. They learnt from one another. It was functioning like a private company then. The management style of functioning was very transparent, fast and innovative. We encouraged suggestions from the staff. The phone-in-programme that had begun on 'All India Radio' (AIR) was later started on *Doordarshan* too. The whole agenda of APDRP was implemented. The overloading of lines was curbed by proposing new lines. By and large massive developmental work happened during my tenure in the KPTCL.

Motivating the Employees

I travelled the entire state and met the employees at district and taluk level. Many times the employees work under stress. We motivated them and redressed their problems. On the whole, the KPTCL term was very satisfying because I had the previous experience of working in the KEB, BESCOM and I was also the chairman of the SCOMs. I knew the total picture of the sector. So, Karnataka's position in terms of improvement in system was very good.

Creation of Rural Feeder

KPTCL is bulk supplier of power to the SCOMs. We have to ration the supply, because of perpetual shortage of electricity. In urban areas, we could not disconnect the power for long, as the consumers there are in the paying category. In rural areas also, it has to be supplied during the peak hours in the morning and evening. That we did. Earlier there was no separate mechanism to ensure supply of electricity to the rural areas. So, we focused on segregation of lines as Gujarat has done on a large scale. By creating rural feeder, we ensured round the clock single phase power to rural areas. Three-phase power in rural areas, which is required to run the pump sets, etc. can be given only for limited hours due to shortage of power. But at least single phase electricity should be provided to them. We had introduced that system in BESCOM and other areas too. The condition of BESCOM in Mangalore and Mysore was better, but Gulbarga and Hubli had lots of problems. Under the APDRP, we got lots of funds for improving the infrastructure there. We upgraded the network and created many new stations there.

How the Power System Works

During the peak hours, there is a shortage of power, as everybody wants power in that duration. There is no problem at the night because most families switch off the lights then and the demand is very low. Most people do not know how the power system works. Power floats in the grid round-the-clock and all grids are interconnected. No grid is isolated. Power in HT or 400 KV lines is already flowing everywhere. These lines are connected to the national grid. Secondly, someone who draws more power has to pay more. During the peak hours the tariff is different i.e. higher. This was done to basically discourage the people to use more power during that time. But some people draw at any cost. A discipline has to be maintained. If we don't disconnect power supply, then there could be a problem. When there is more power in the system, you have to switch-off the generating system. Because you cannot go on pumping, the entire system will burst. There is no way of storing power. It has to be used when it is required. It is a very technical subject in that sense. We have to maintain a balance between the hydro and thermal power also. We use hydro power during the peak hours. Afterwards its generation is switched off. If we continue the generation, the water goes waste, which nobody can afford. It is a technical subject and requires lot of care at all fronts.

□

CURBING PILFERAGE IN WELFARE FUNDS

Leakage in welfare funds meant for the deprived sections of the society has been a major concern since decades. Former Prime Minister Rajiv Gandhi during the Eighties had said that only 17 paisa reaches the real beneficiary. Instead of any improvement, the situation only worsened as the former Deputy Chairman of Planning Commission claimed on October 14, 2009 that 'only 16 paisa reaches the beneficiary'. With the objective of re-engineering the existing delivery process in welfare schemes, for faster flow of funds and to ensure accurate targeting of the beneficiaries, de-duplication and reduction of fraud, the Direct Benefit Transfer (DBT) was introduced on January 1, 2013. Under First phase, it was initiated in 43 districts, and later on 78 more districts were added in 27 schemes pertaining to scholarships, women, child and labour welfare. It was expanded across the country on December 12, 2014. Seven new scholarship schemes and Mahatma Gandhi National Rural Employment Guarantee Act (MGNREGA) were brought under it in 300 identified districts.

Now Electronic Payment Framework, laid down in February 2015, has to be followed by all Departments and their attached Institutions, and it is applicable to all Central Sector or Centrally Sponsored Schemes where components of cash is transferred to individual beneficiaries. As on November 2016, over 25 crore Jan Dhan Accounts, over 108 crore Aadhaar cards and more than 103 crore Mobile phone connections provide a unique opportunity to bring more efficiency, effectiveness, transparency and accountability in the Government system and infuse confidence of citizens in governance.

Dignified Life to Socially Disadvantaged

Secretary, Social Welfare Department, from June 2008 to June 2009

Social Welfare Department was the first Department where I was posted in Secretariat after lot of field postings in June 2008. Of course, I had taken up assignments in the form of implementation of SCSP/TSP components (Scheduled Castes Sub-plan and Tribal Sub-Plan). In those days, the Social Welfare Department also used to have schemes for welfare of Backward Classes. Only minority welfare was separate. Subsequently, the Department was bifurcated.

When I joined the Department as Secretary, we were flooded with complaints related to the quality of services and overall management of hostels meant for SC/ST students. Even outsiders stayed in those hostels in large numbers. After joining the Department, I searched for the guidelines for hostels and the duties and responsibilities of hostel wardens. To my surprise, there were no such guidelines. So, immediately we decided to formulate guidelines and subsequently prepared a booklet detailing all the relevant information.

Largest Training Group

The staff members of the Departments were never exposed to any training. All staff put together, there were around 14,000 employees. We decided to train all of them about their duties and responsibilities. We organised one-day training for them using the satellite network of Abdul

Nazir Sab State Institute for Rural Development and Panchayati Raj. We called all the employees at block level and connected to them through satellite. The then Minister of Social Welfare also addressed the employees. We had lot of interaction with them. At the end, they were very happy to learn certain things during the training. It was for the first time that all the 14,000 employees were imparted training in one go. That was a huge motivation for them.

Simultaneously, we also started holding grievance meetings with the SC/ST organisations. We reviewed the SCSP/TSP and also reviewed the grants by other departments. We also persuaded the government to increase the budget allocation. Since Social Welfare Department was the nodal agency for implementation of welfare schemes, we get grants from other departments as well. But we noticed that the beneficiary oriented schemes funded by various corporations were not being implemented properly. There was a severe problem of middlemen.

Central Procurement of Things

The Department gets huge funds from the Government, but the delivery of services in hostels was a big challenge. It was seen that good quality stuff was not being provided—substandard equipments and food items were being purchased. Following all these problems, we centralised the procurement at district level. We allowed the hostel wardens to procure certain things up to Rs. one lakh at local level. No tender was required to purchase certain things like milk, vegetables, foodgrains, etc. We introduced many such reforms. There definitely was some initial opposition to these reforms. But before the people who opposed came to know about those reforms I got the formal orders issued. If you hold somebody responsible at local level, you have to give him/her some powers too. Both, the hostel wardens and the students were happy with those reforms, because the wardens got some power and the students got healthier meals.

Non-Stop 25-Days Tour of the State

In order to understand the ground realities and to

exhort the machinery, I toured the entire state covering all the districts in 25 days. The tour was non-stop. During the tour, I had discussions with the officials and ground level staff at district, taluk and block levels. I called them at different places and sensitised. I emphasised that the Human Development Index (HDI) cannot change unless we impart good quality education to the young generation and ensure healthcare facilities to the people. In fact, that is what we lack in real sense. The Hyderabad Karnataka region, which comprises of Bidar, Yadgir, Raichur, Koppal, Bellary and Gulbarga, was the worst hit in that sense.

Showing Results on the Ground

I sensitised the officials that if the budget is spent, then improvement must also happen on the ground over a period of time. The situation must have changed after six decades of the Independence, but that was not happening in some regions. To our surprise, many officers did not know anything about the HDI—what are its components, how is it calculated, what is the ranking of their districts in HDI, etc. Though the state government had already prepared and distributed a document in this regard, they were not aware of that. Then we used to show them their HDI index. It was a very interesting interaction—more of a reviewing meeting than educating them.

Surprise Visits to Hostels

By and large, the experience in Social Welfare Department was quite fulfilling and activity centric. We conducted surprise visits to hostels, shared food with the students, interacted with them and sought their suggestions. We also put up some inspirational slogans in the hostels. We tried to ensure that both the Superintendents and Wardens have a feeling of ownership towards the hostels. At many places, a positive change was observed. Through all these efforts, we could minimise and eventually eliminate disparity between the people belonging to socially disadvantaged categories and thereby enabled them to lead a productive and dignified life.

□

BEAUTIFICATION OF CITIES

The 'Swachh Survekshan 2016', conducted by the Government of India under the Swachh Bharat Mission, declared Mysuru (Karnataka) as the cleanest city of India. Chandigarh and Tiruchirapalli (Tamil Nadu) were ranked as second and third respectively. The survey covered 476 cities. The same survey also prepared the list of dirtiest cities. Dhanbad in Jharkhand was found to be the dirtiest city. Asansol in West Bengal is second dirtiest and Itanagar in Arunachal Pradesh is third dirtiest city. Similarly, Patna in Bihar, Meerut in Uttar Pradesh, Raipur in Chhattisgarh, Ghaziabad in Uttar Pradesh, Jamshedpur in Jharkhand, Varanasi in Uttar Pradesh and Kalyan Dombivli in Maharashtra are the other dirtiest cities in the list of top 10 dirtiest cities. The survey was commissioned by the Ministry of Urban Development to review the sanitation and hygiene conditions in 75 major municipalities, including 53 cities with a population of above 10 lakh each and the state capitals. The survey commenced on January 5, 2016.

Swachh Bharat Abhiyan, conceptualised by Prime Minister Narendra Modi, definitely sensitised people about cleanliness, but other than cleaning the streets the cleanliness in a city also has many other components like graffiti, cinema posters, hoardings, banners, pamphlets, etc. There is a law in almost every city to prevent people from defacing the city; however, it is hardly implemented effectively. In such a situation, the big question is 'how to keep the cities clean?' In such a situation, Bengaluru, where walls have been painted with fascinating paintings related to Kannada heritage, tourism, culture, great personalities, etc shows the way ahead.

Mesmerising Wall Art

Materialising an Innovative Idea to get rid of the Defaced Walls in Cities as Commissioner of Bruhat Bangalore Mahanagara Palike from June 2009 to June 2010

I got the news of my posting to Bruhat Bangalore Mahanagara Palike (BBMP) in June 2009 when I was interacting with the people at Ankalagi village in Bagalkot District. The interaction was about making Ankalagi a model village. Other officers of the District were also there and it was a serious discussion with the villagers. During the discussion, I got the news to come and take the charge of BBMP. I went to Bangalore, but was told not to take the charge. I said, OK. I believe some MLAs had called up the Chief Minister requesting him not to post a strict officer like me in BBMP, as it would be very difficult for them to draw 'benefits'. As usual, I went back to Mangalore to continue my inspection and hold further meetings. The Chief Minister was to visit Mangalore shortly. MLAs would have met him, but even then, after the CM's tour, I received instructions to join the BBMP. Hence, I reported there.

Cleanliness was Top Priority

The immediate task in my mind was to have some impact

on the cleanliness part in the city—cleanliness in terms of waste management, total upkeeps of walls, public places, etc. The ugly sights of cinema posters, pamphlets affixed on the walls, slogan writings, etc. were there throughout the city. It was more visible on the main roads giving very poor impression about the whole city. I had already seen some cities in the UK with fascinating paintings and murals. Therefore, I thought to take up a drive to remove all the ugly cinema posters and make those places attractive so that people do not deface them again.

I discussed the idea with the officers whether it should be done or not, and if it should be then, how. They agreed. Then the question was what to be done, as after cleaning the walls the people may again put posters or indulge in graffiti. Then the idea came to paint something educating and fascinating portraying the cultural heritage of the state.

Fascinating Paintings on the Walls

Hence, we decided to take up the main roads—arterial roads connecting the city with outside. We identified all such roads and converted them into different themes. Like, if one goes to Bannerghatta National Park, it has to have a wildlife theme. The Road, which leads to Mysore should show heritage of Mysore. If it leads to NH4 or Tumkur side, it has to be the entire state of Karnataka. Equally, if it goes to Hasan side, it has to be coastal regions of Halebidu and Malnad, etc. This is how we identified the areas and the themes for paintings. Then the question arose as to who will undertake it and which officers would supervise. We found lots of painters who earlier painted cinema posters and were then jobless due to advancements in printing technology. Our officers looked for them, brought them and showed them the photos to be painted. They said they would easily paint them. That is how the idea of painting was materialised. We adequately paid them for this task.

There is a very popular hoarding opposite UB City on Cubbon Park, which usually shows public interest posters. It is one of the prime attractions in Bangalore because of the educating and motivating slogans. All the slogans written there over the years were collected from the owner. Then we also collected material from the Tourism Department and some other sources. The work was started after full ground work. Through this project, the jobless painters got the work. Then emerged the question of cinema posters—where to allow them. We strictly told the cinema owners not to paste the posters anywhere in the city. They would seek permission and then the space for them would be erected separately. We identified about 100 places for them to paste the posters. The decision was taken after consulting them. We basically auctioned those places for posters. Even then there were some people, who violated the norms. We filed police cases against them. They tried to pressurise us through various methods and also sent delegations, but finally they had to agree to put posters at the designated places only.

Increased Awareness among Children

Apart from converting the ugly sights into fascinating places, an interesting outcome of the entire drive was increased awareness among children about the places painted on the walls. Many children inquired their parents about those places and also insisted to visit them during holidays. A professor, Dr. Pratibha Singh from Karnataka Chitrakala Parishath, wrote a book on the entire drive. Since the news about the experiment was carried by the international media, a lady from a foreign country conducted research on the project. In Chennai, the Corporation passed a resolution to follow it in the city. It created a very good vibe about the total initiative. It was appreciated by many. Of course, there were some people who, instead of appreciating, opposed it.

Mass Movement in Shimoga

It was for the first time that such a drive was taken up for cleanliness and was done on such a large scale. Apart from Chennai, some other cities also copied it. Many of our own cities in Karnataka like Belgaum and Channagiri also imitated it. Then some schools took up. Shimoga took it up in mass mode.

By and large, it was a nice experience. Some people opposed saying it is not aesthetics or we were not consulted before doing it. All those were baseless arguments. If action has to be taken, it has to be taken. At some places the paintings are still good. Karnataka Brihad Pradhikar has written a letter to the Chief Secretary to revive these paintings and continue the experiment. The orders to revive these paintings have been passed recently. Hope, they would be preserved or redrawn.

Generating the Sense and Belongingness

Wall Art was an idea to get rid of the ugly walls, a big headache for every small or big city. However, there are laws in every city to curb defacing of walls, the civic sense of majority urban people is so poor that they scarcely think of the beauty of their city, while indulging in defacing the public property. Without adequate civic sense, no civic agency can ensure cleanliness in the city. The public has to be engaged by generating a sense of belongingness. We tried to do that by painting some walls in Bangalore with the paintings of the State's rich heritage or the great personalities. That is why it was noticed at nowhere that anyone defaced those walls again. The idea clicked. It proved highly educating for the children and also those coming from outside. For tourism point of view too it was appreciated.

□

DISPOSAL OF WASTE

Every Indian city seems to be struggling hard to cope with managing the waste output. When it comes to waste management, little is done. Metro cities and major economic hubs generate the maximum volume of waste. A survey of 20 smaller cities selected to be developed as smart cities shows that most of them struggle to manage waste. Waste management is surely a global problem, but it is not tackled in India as seriously as it is done in other countries. Around 4.7 million tonnes of garbage is generated all over the world daily, which is expected to rise up to 6 million tonnes by 2025. According to Central Pollution Control Board (CPCB) data, India generates .4 million tonnes waste daily and only 83% of it is collected. And, only 29% of the collected waste is treated. Delhi daily generates 8,390 tonnes waste, Mumbai 11,000 tonnes, Chennai 4,800 tonnes, Bengaluru 3,500 tonnes and Kolkata 4,000 tonnes.

The Municipal Solid Wastes (Management and Handling) Rules, 2000 provides detailed specifications for collection, segregation, storage, transportation, processing and disposal of the waste. This includes directives to municipal authorities to organise awareness programmes for citizens to encourage segregation and recycling. Experts have been pushing for segregation at source and feel a strict framework of laws and the fear of penalty is needed to make people comply. In fact, whatever little recycling is happening in our cities is because of the waste pickers, who recycle about 20-25% of the waste. We need to learn from Sweden, which is a zero waste country and Sri Lanka, which segregates its waste with perfection.

Model of Scientific Waste Management

Collection, transportation and disposal of waste is a big challenge for any urban body. Bruhat Bengaluru Mahanagara Palike (BBMP) too is no different. Since every house and individual generates waste round the clock, waste management is relevant 24×7. It has to be collected, cleaned and disposed of to a satisfactory level every day.

When I took over as Commissioner of BBMP in June 2009, right from day one, I focused on cleanliness. I visited all the sites where the waste was dumped and disposed of, including Doddaballapura, where a private person had put up a plant. During those visits, I noticed that cleaning was proper in some areas, but in some areas it was grossly unsatisfactory. When I searched for the reasons, I found that the contractors, instead of disposing of the waste from those areas, just dumped it here and there. I went into the details of it and to my utter surprise found there were no written orders as to which contractor would dispose of the waste at which place. Wherever they found a convenient place, they dumped it. In some cases, they had purchased private lands to dump the waste, which was unauthorised as well as the land was insufficient.

GPS on Waste Carrying Vehicles

Then we worked out a schedule—ward wise and

contractor wise—and specifically fixed the sites and decided who will dump the waste where. We also put up a weighing machine at every entry point of the dumping yards equipped with CCTV cameras, which helped us find which lorry came at what time and how much weight it carried. We also installed GPS on every lorry to strengthen the system. However, initially there was resistance from the contractors, they agreed when we clearly declined any compromise over it. As the lorry passed, it automatically got uploaded in the system. It helped us in effective monitoring—how many Lorries are plying on the road on a particular day, who is the contractor, where is it being dumped, etc.

Earlier, in some areas, BBMP used local tractors, which carried small quantity of waste. Back then the tendering process was also confusing. We streamlined the process, but it was strongly opposed by the contractors. There was apparently a nexus between the contractors, local officials and some of the political leaders. The exact number of trips they actually made and the number of trips shown on paper were different. That is how they made money. The rate that they had quoted on competitive basis was also not viable. But they made money by showing the fake tractor trips. Without making the entire waste disposal mechanism automatic—from household to every vehicle through GPS, tracking was difficult. But we did it successfully.

Segregation of the Waste

Segregation has proved to be highly useful in effective disposal of the waste. Some NGOs in Malleswaram and other parts of the city were doing a good job on this front. We started training and organising awareness programmes through them in other areas too. It proved that waste can properly be handled and it is not a loss-making proposition. If we segregate dry waste from the wet waste, 90% dry waste can be reused or recycled. It does not need to be collected every day. Even if 60% of the bulk is dry waste and if it is properly segregated, it can be stored at different levels. Then depending upon their needs, people can procure it. It is possible. In some areas like Vellore, 100% segregation and scientific disposal of waste has been possible.

The involvement of public in any initiative is essential. If they don't segregate the waste inside their houses, the system cannot work. The dry and wet waste should be collected separately. In some areas, it was seen that in houses, the waste was segregated, but the persons collecting that mixed it again. In that situation, it does not serve the purpose and all efforts went wasted. We tried to educate the people at all levels. Segregation is the solution.

We made efforts to acquire about 2000 acres more government land for the dumping yards around Bangalore. But could not succeed for some reasons. We were told to give in writing that the waste would not be dumped here and there. No municipal authority can give any such undertaking. It has to be dumped somewhere and a place has to be found where it can be disposed of scientifically. Waste is the thing that everybody wants to discard. Everybody generates waste, but nobody wants it to be close to one's house. That is the general tendency.

Manure from Green Waste

In some market areas, we introduced the system of producing manure from the green waste—vegetable waste, etc. There are machines, which convert this waste into manure quickly. We introduced it in Malleshwaram market. Another major initiative was building of segregation points in every ward. We ordered for building such points in about 100 wards. We identified land for it and started building the collection centres. Such points should be there in every ward.

Camera on Each Vehicle

In case of wet waste also we can adopt different methods. The wet waste in hotels is basically food, which can be fed to animals. It does not need to be mixed with other waste. The dry waste in markets can also be tackled separately. By and large, a comprehensive and integrated strategy can help resolve this problem. During my tenure, we deputed a chief engineer for waste management and generating awareness. We also installed a camera on each vehicle. We could record the movement of the vehicle. This helped detect the waste lying anywhere and also check if the street lights were on during day time. We also ensured that the waste was disposed of during night only and no vehicle moved openly. In Gandhi Nagar area, one Joint Commissioner had taken this initiative. They had introduced twenty-four hour cleaning. Normally, cleaning is done only once. But there it was done thrice a day. They kept drums and boxes at several points. The initiative got citizens award also from the Governor for this noble contribution.

Cleanliness for Health

All these efforts prove that despite Bangalore being a metropolitan city, it is possible to manage it effectively. After I left the Department, a survey was conducted and Mysore was found to be the cleanest city in the state. But in Metro cities, Bangalore was on top in terms of cleanliness. That has to be kept up. It is the main function of an urban body. The Government of India launched Swachh Bharat Abhiyan in 2014, but we tried to create a model for urban cleanliness years ago. Cleanliness requires change in the mindset. If the people cooperate with the civic bodies, 50% cleanliness can be ensured without investing even a single penny.

It is good that people all over the country are gradually getting more aware of the cleanliness, especially after the launch of Swachh Bharat Abhiyan by Prime Minister

Mr. Narendra Modi. Cleanliness is essential not only for beautification of our locality, but more than that for our own health. That has to be understood. Every road, path, office, home, hut, stream and particle of air around us has to be kept clean. We must change the mindset that cleaning is the responsibility of the civic employees (sweepers) alone. Every citizen has a role in it. It is everybody's responsibility. □

BBMP Welfare Schemes and Reforms

Being a public institution, the Bruhat Bengaluru Mahanagara Palike's (BBMP) is bound by certain requirements of the law. It has to spend 22% of the grants for welfare of SC/STs, undertake some housing schemes, and maintain hospitals and schools. These schemes were already there, but the quality of services particularly in hospitals and schools was not satisfactory at all. I decided to emphasise on it during my tenure as Commissioner in 2009.

Schools

In order to improve the quality of education in BBMP schools, we took the help of Department of Public Instruction (DDPI). The students in those schools are mainly from the economically weaker sections of the society. Logistics was not an issue, as buildings were already there. Quality of teachers, inputs, training to them was essential and we did that.

Hospitals

Maximum number of pregnancy treatments and deliveries happen in the BBMP hospitals only. Again 99% of the patients coming there are from the poorer sections. Even people from rural areas visit them for deliveries. The hospital upkeep and management was a big issue for the Corporation employees. The level of commitment had to be very high. Dispensation of medicines and upgradation of hospital was also a challenge. We took up all these issues systematically and provided adequate budgets for the hospitals. Though they are small hospitals, they serve the large sections of the society. My emphasis was on budget hike and training to the hospital staff. That was enough to have good upkeep of the hospitals.

Houses to Homeless

During my tenure I noticed that the funds under Special Component Plan for SCs and Tribal Sub Plan (SCP/TSP) were unspent for a long time. Under this plan, all governments have to allocate a percentage of their budget for the welfare of SC/STs. This allocation has to be proportionate to the population of SC/STs in that area. For example, 22.75% of Karnataka's population is SC/STs; hence 22.75% of the budgets in the state, including that of BBMP, should be for SC/STs. When enquired, the officers gave several excuses for their inefficiency. If the budget is provided, it has to be spent. Normally, we don't see slums in Bangalore. But the metro city had more than 500 slums where we needed to improve the living standard of people by providing them basic amenities. There too the funds could be spent. The reconstruction of individual houses, which are outside the slums, can also be done with the BBMP assistance.

The backlog of unspent SCP/TSP funds was ₹ 250 crore. I decided to spend that fund for housing, which is a major requirement of life. If one has a house, it helps the family permanently. I asked the Joint Commissioners to list the beneficiaries wherever they find. I gave them the target of 10,000 houses to be built in slums. It was taken up as a mission, and in a short span, we could provide houses to thousands of needy families. I personally visited many houses and localities and the public response was overwhelming. We also took the help of bankers, HUDCO,

Urban Ashraya and Department of Slum Development for assistance.

Dengue fever, cleaning of drains and over-flowing drain water are other major issues. We addressed them too. We also provided uniform to students, individual benefits to different communities, building their community halls, etc. Although welfare schemes were there, the money had not been spent for the last three years. Because it was Administrator's period during my tenure, I could take easy decisions and spend the money without any undue interference.

Computerisation of Advertisement Sites

Taxes and advertisements are the major source, of revenue for BBMP. However, leakage in advertisement revenue was a big challenge. We curbed it effectively by computerising all the advertisement sites and finally generated more revenue from it. We also generated revenue by introducing B Khatas for the houses, which were complete and people were occupying but the commencement certificate had not been issued. Shortage of funds is a never-ending phenomenon there, because the BBMP activities cannot be self-sustaining. Hence, we got some budgetary support from the state government for constructing and upgrading the roads, etc.

Four-Lane Roads

Another major plan that we executed in the BBMP was upgrading the roads and making them four-laned by utilising the Transfer of Development Rights (TDRs) scheme. Commissioner was authorised for that. We identified some arterial and sub-arterial roads—main roads which connect the city and the roads which connect from one arterial road to another arterial road. About 800 km length of roads was identified. We planned four lanes for a number of areas. But for doing it we required people's consent. We could obtain the consent of about 20% people. We had also called for tenders for execution of the work. But soon the elected body assumed charge and decided not to go ahead with road widening. Some people also challenged the tenders that we had invited. Some even went to court, which finally ruled that there was nothing wrong in the tender process. In fact, there was no will in the elected body to complete the project. If we had 800 km four-lane roads in Bangalore, it would have eased the traffic movement. But easy movement of traffic is nobody's business. The project was to be completed in two years and we had arranged sufficient funds also from various agencies.

Multi-level Parking

Parking issues are always there in any metro city. We decided to build multi-level and underground parking facilities. An officer requires full support from the government to transform the city. It is not difficult. The main issue is of garbage collection, disposable, transportation, ease of traffic movement. If all these are done efficiently there is nothing wrong in a city. Plans should be there, because development follows the planning. But that does not normally happen in our Indian cities.

Corruption is a common issue everywhere. We can effectively curb it with the help of digital technology. If the file movement is online, then tracking files becomes very easy and the chances of their unnecessary delay are minimised. Urban planning needs collective efforts. No fruitful result would be achieved until the whole process is guided by visionaries in the elected bodies. Once the combination is there, miraculous results can be achieved.

□

VANISHING TRADITIONAL WATER BODIES

In a hurry to expand cities the people have already eaten into the traditional water bodies i.e. lakes, ponds, etc which not only help in flood control, but also contribute in a big way towards groundwater recharge. A survey conducted in 2014 by Delhi Parks and Gardens Society reveals that out of 611 water bodies in Delhi, 274 have already dried up and as many as 190 cannot be revived anymore. A 2012 study exposed that out of about 650 small and big water bodies, Chennai now has less than 30 bodies, and the area of 19 major lakes has shrunk from a total of 1,130 hectares (ha) to 645 ha. Hyderabad, too, has lost 3,245 ha area of its water bodies in the last 15 years. In 1960s, Bengaluru had 280 interlinked tanks, which reduced to less than 80 in 1993. New Delhi based Centre for Science and Environment (CSE) in its study found that in 2001, 137 lakes were listed in Ahmadabad, but, by 2012, 65 were already destroyed and built upon.

As the groundwater level dips, cities are sourcing their water from hundreds of kilometers away. Jodhpur sources water from Indira Gandhi Canal, which is 205 km away. Mumbai's water supply comes from dams and lakes over 120 km away. Chennai's water is sourced from Veeranam Lake, some 200 km away. Hyderabad gets its water supply from Krishna River 116 km away. No wonder the agencies have to spend about 30-50% of their funds on electricity to pump water, while almost 30-50% of the water is 'lost' in leakages. If we fail to arrest our shrinking traditional water bodies, the smart cities will only end up digging their watery graves.

Balancing Lakes and City Development

When I was posted in Bruhat Bangalore Mahanagara Palike (BBMP), the condition of traditional lakes and tanks was very pathetic. Lakes were fast vanishing from the 'Lake City' due to encroachment and negligence on the part of the agencies concerned. It is widely believed that prominent developers in Bangalore are the major encroachers of the the water bodies beds. They have encroached lakes and tanks on large scale in rural Bangalore too. Armed with the Belgaum experience of lake development, I spoke to the Chief Secretary and got the lakes transferred to BBMP. Then we got all the lakes surveyed, identified the areas under encroachment and started removing the encroachment from lakes. The move was obviously not unopposed. Lot of resistance was there. But once we took the decision, we did not come under any pressure.

Making Drains Encroachment-Free

Apart from restoring the lakes, my second emphasis was to remove the encroachment from storm water drains (SWDs). It was a must to prevent flooding in the city during rains. About 2,000 storm water drains were under encroachment. There are four major valleys in the city, which drain Bangalore. During rains many areas get flooded. Several years back, the city witnessed so much rain that many houses got washed away. At one place on Mysore Road, when I went there, I found a family trapped inside the house. They had locked the door, but water entered the house and the family found no way to come out. The house was just facing the drain. As we somehow opened the door, the family was about to wash away in heavy flow of water. I myself caught hold of them along with others. We had to struggle hard to rescue the family. We continued to receive calls from the public and the MLAs for rescue from various areas. We sent teams and saved the lives of people. Relief operations for the flood victims were also started.

Restoring 500 Year Old Kempambudhi Tank

There has been a healthy balance between the lakes and city development. We wanted to restore that balance. That is why we took up the survey, identified the sites under encroachment and removed it. Then we did channelling and fencing of all the lakes to ensure there is no further encroachment. Whatever channelling and fencing of lakes is seen today happened during that time only. I have the satisfaction that I could save some of the lakes in Bangalore. Otherwise, most of them would have vanished by now. Lakes are very much part of the city life. They also enhance beauty of the city. After removing encroachment, we focused on developmental work around those lakes. It increased the real estate prices in those areas, because the public loves to live near water bodies. I sanctioned Rs. five crore for renovation of Kempambudhi Tank, built by the founder of Bangalore, the late Kempe Gowda. That 500 year old tank was also restored during that period. This way most lakes were restored in the city.

The builder lobby plays a key role in encroachment of lakes and tanks by adopting various means. They cover the lakes and sell the property on high rates. That lobby however tried to pressurise us through different methods, but I did not stop the lake restoration work. Some people living in slums around the lakes requested us to make alternate arrangements. We thought over their request sympathetically. Demolition of slums takes time, because you cannot make those deprived people homeless. Making them homeless was not our purpose. But the individual houses were removed. In Yalhanka, below the tank there is lot of land, which we wanted to develop as another source of water. If the lake is restored down below, they get recharged. They have link from one to another. If proper water goes there it helps greatly in recharging.

Arresting Sewage Flow in Lakes

The major cause of worry for us was that sewage water was going into the lakes uninterrupted. Many lakes including famous Ulsoor Lake received huge quantity of sewage water. Hence, bifurcation of sewage water was another priority. Most of the sewage pipelines have been laid below the lake bed. Therefore, water gets mixed up. To curb that was another priority area. In slum areas, we planned to build individual toilets and connecting them with the underground drainage system. Sanitation management is itself a big task in cities. It is bigger than the waste management. So many issues are involved in it, which we normally do not realise.

Sustained Efforts Required

In Western countries, the whole sewage system is below the houses and roads. There is parallel system there. Big nullahs are also there and the drain water is pushed in that system. But in Bangalore, it is not like that. It cannot go underground because of rocks. The best way to drain it is to put it down, flush it and let it go outside. Then flooding does not happen. In Bangalore, floods happen because, as it rains, it immediately fills up the drains. In the good old days, it drained slowly, because many lakes were there and they absorbed whatever water came and it took lot of time for them to overflow. By the time it overflew, the other water was already drained off. But today, houses have come up everywhere. It is mostly a concrete jungle. Whatever water pours down during rains, immediately flows into the drain. Since drain capacity is not increased, so it floods. Silting is also there. All these issues create a headache. We tried to take some steps to reduce this headache. But this work could not be done overnight. It requires sustained efforts.

□

Rejuvenating Lakes in the Lake City

Bangalore is famous as City of Lakes. People say there were thousands of lakes in the city in the greater region of Bangalore. More than 100 lakes in and around Bangalore were said to be built by the founder of Bangalore, Kempe Gowda and his successors. Most lakes were constructed by damming the natural valley systems by constructing bunds. They met the drinking water and irrigation needs of the community and were known to have a positive impact on the ecology and microclimate of the city. They not only helped by replenishing the groundwater resources in the vicinity, but also prevented flooding, treated wastewater, arrested the sediment loads and functioned as a productive ecosystem. Tanks were built both in rural and urban areas for catering to the multiple needs of the people. Compared to other cities in the state, a number of lakes and tanks were built in and around Bangalore. That is why it is known as the city of lakes or air-conditioned city of South India.

Disappearing Lakes

There are many places in the city where originally there were lakes. For example, the Kempe Gowda Bus Stand was built over a lake. Sree Kanteevara Stadium has also been built over a lake bed. It shows the city had no other space and the lakes were not spare. During my tenure in the BBMP, I noticed that besides the government projects, many lakes were encroached by general public too. Firstly, the lakes are used as dumping ground. Once they are filled up, they are encroached upon to settle on them. Many slums and individual houses have come up on several lakes in the similar fashion.

Taking over Remaining Lakes for Rejuvenation

The Lake Development Authority had to control the encroachment of lakes. But the Authority was ineffective due to various reasons including shortage of staff and funds, etc. I proposed if the Lake Development Authority cannot preserve the lakes, why not hand them over to the BBMP. During meetings, they said it is up to the Chief Secretary to take a decision in this regard. Then I wrote to the Chief Secretary requesting him to convene a meeting on the issue calling all concerned agencies. I proposed to hand over all lakes to the BBMP, because only then it will be able to spend money for their rejuvenation and development. Since there was no elected body in the BBMP then, and the Administrator was free to take decisions, I took decisions without any hurdle. The Chief Secretary convened a meeting and decided to hand over the lakes to us. Except 8-9 lakes with the Lake Development Authority and Forest Department, rest of the lakes were handed over to the BBMP.

Removing Encroachment

About 183 lakes were there in the city then. I immediately conducted a survey of all the live lakes. Then we identified the area under encroachment and started acting against the encroachers. Once the encroachment was cleared, we did immediate channelling and fencing. Today, whatever channelling and fencing people see around lakes in Bangalore was done back then only. I made a Chief

Engineer fully in-charge of lake development cell. Then the construction work and plantation was started along the periphery so that there is no further encroachment. Then subsequently about a dozen lakes were given to the BDA, which developed them. The development of remaining lakes was done by the BBMP. We earmarked lots of funds for lake development.

Acclamation from High Court

The preservation and rejuvenation of lakes is very necessary. It has to be done everywhere. When I was in Belgaum, I found the famous Belgaum Tank in the city was under encroachment. It was to be breached and converted into commercial as well as residential sites. The lakes, when dried, follow the same pattern everywhere. I used the experience of Belgaum in Bangalore. However, I did not involve the public in restoration work at Bangalore; we aggressively went ahead, surveyed the encroachment, identified it and removed it. Resistance was there at some places, but legally they could not do anything. Finally, we rescued those lakes. I am happy that the Lake Development Cell continues to exist. The Bangalore High Court had also taken cognizance of it and said the lakes must be preserved.

Rejuvenation of Drains

After lakes, we focused on rejuvenation of the drains, because removal of encroachment from the drains was another major issue. We may have lakes, if water flow is not there, they are bound to get encroached upon. In order to ensure proper flow in the drains, we removed encroachment from the drains. We cleared all the storm water drains in all the wards. At some places, people had put pillars and bridged the drain to build houses. We removed all of them. At several places, there were even three or four story houses that we had to demolish in City Centre Gandhi Nagar area. It was stupendous task.

The Commissioner's job is of 24 hours. There are no office timings. My day began with sunrise and by that time I used to be in the field. That time traffic was also little lesser, we could meet lots of people during morning walks, know their problems, then come back and attend the office. That was my routine. Normally, the officers are not happy if you make them wake up early and make them go to the field. But, they must face the public and answer them. I was not alone to answer, they too had to answer. If I myself went to the field, they realised there was no option for them but to go to the field.

□

URBAN EXPLOSION

The urban explosion is taking a toll on the green coverage. As a result, the quality of air and water is degrading. Cities have become the source of many dangerous gases, because vehicles like passenger cars, Lorries, buses, etc. generate carbon dioxide (CO_2), carbon monoxide (CO), sulphur dioxide (SO_2), nitrous oxides (Nox), benzene, creating serious threat to human health.

A study conducted by Indian Institute of Science's Centre for Ecological Sciences in 2013 revealed that Kolkata's tree cover, a third of its area in 1980, is likely to fall to 3.37% by 2030. Similarly, Ahmadabad's tree cover, from 45% of its area in 1970, is likely to fall to 3% by 2030. Bhopal's tree cover, from 67% in 1992, to a likely 11% by 2030. Bengaluru's condition is the worst over years, where during the four decades, vegetation has declined 66%. Similarly, Hyderabad's tree cover fell from 2.71% to 1.66% over 20 years. The UN predicts an urban growth rate of 62% between 2010 and 2020; 108% between 2020 and 2030. Therefore, the urban planners have to maintain at least 33% green cover in cities.

Trees in the urban system provide a variety of ecosystem services including biodiversity conservation, removal of atmospheric pollutants, oxygen generation, noise reduction, mitigation of urban heat island effect, microclimate regulation, stabilisation of soil, groundwater recharge, prevention of soil erosion and carbon sequestration. International minimum standard, suggested by WHO, requires a minimum availability of 9 square meters of green open space per city dweller. Hence, the city planners need to take into consideration the action and the initiatives required in advance to ensure proper greening.

Creating Green Garland Around the Garden City

Commissioner Bangalore Development Authority from June 2010 to June 2012

From BBMP, I moved to Bangalore Development Authority (BDA) in June 2010 as Commissioner. I had a good background of working in the BBMP, but there is fundamental difference in working of both the Departments. BBMP mainly deals with the civic issues—collection of waste, maintenance of street lights, roads, etc, whereas in BDA one is concerned mostly with the allotees—the people whom sites have been allotted. Compared to BDA, people have more interaction with the BBMP. Both the departments are complementary to each other. Sometimes there were discussions as to why both these departments are separate.

Formulating Master Plan

The difference in both the Departments is that the BBMP has smaller area than the BDA. The Development Authority is for a larger area. As the city grows, the peripheral area also impacts the urban development. So, there has to be planned growth, because that area is also going to become urban area in times to come. Therefore, the mandate of the BDA is to prepare a Master Plan for the city—both the main city and the peripheral area—the extended areas. The Master Plan is normally prepared for longer periods like

20 to 30 years detailing out the growth that should happen and where. It is done by BDA, because the BBMP has no mandate for it. BBMP only has to sanction buildings as per the Master Plan. In case of high-rise buildings, BDA has to approve the plans in city areas.

Problems in Implementation of the Master Plan

The BDA is supposed to develop infrastructure including the roads, etc. Theoretically, it is believed that if developed area comes to the city, problems are less. But in practice it doesn't happen so. I also realised it. We made many Master Plans. Roads, parks, civic amenities, etc. were all indicated in the Plan. But during implementation it doesn't happen. All the roads shown in the Master Plan are hardly seen on the ground. Only the areas, built or developed by the developers, get developed. Other areas remain neglected. If all the roads are developed, the congestion does not happen. That is what the BDA planning lacks. It makes good plans, but it does not get fully translated into reality. There is a provision. If you don't acquire the land for five years, you cannot implement it. Though we prepare the Master Plan, show the parks, etc, but the BDA does not acquire sufficient land. Without acquiring the land, private rights remain there. After five years, they again do whatever they like. Then the Master Plan undergoes changes and the predefined activities do not take place.

BDA does the major infrastructure development work like the arterial road, big road, fly overs, etc. Sometimes the government mandates the BDA to develop the city areas. For example, in Lalbagh (Bangalore) the BDA spent money in restoration of glass house, lakes and other things. When I was in BBMP, I got 183 lakes under the BBMP. Parts of those lakes were given to BDA for development. The BDA developed the lakes in the outer areas also. It is because the BDA has more resources and it can spend money.

Project of 100 Crore Trees

A major task we planned in the BDA was to take the waste land around nullahs, government lands, government parks, etc. We identified 14,000 acres of such land. We also wrote to the Revenue Department for such land. But the Revenue Department did not hand over the entire land. It wanted to consider on case to case basis. In the Master Plan, we show nullahs but in practice they are narrowed down and buffer is not left out. We wanted to plant saplings on those nullahs. We conceived a green corridor—'Hasrumale' or the green garland around Bangalore.

We had planned to plant one crore saplings in one year. Hence, we prepared for 100 crore plants. We were in search of land and fortunately we got it near Hasargadda and in some other areas as well. Finally, we ended up in planting 30 lakh saplings. Now those plants have grown into big trees, contributing hugely in terms of green cover of the city. I had the idea of ensuring one person one plant. I wanted to plant one sapling on behalf of every citizen of the city. That is how the target of one crore plants was prepared. We also provided budget for it. Limitation of space was there, but we took up big plantation in lake areas, public areas, roadside areas, waterways, etc. That was a big initiative. I am happy that we could plant and nurture about 30 lakh saplings.

Preserving Ecology

The good thing about Bangalore is that wherever you plant a sapling, it grows perfectly because of the good climate, sufficient rainfall and good quality of soil. That is why Bangalore is called a garden city. The same environment concern, which was there in BBMP continued in BDA also.

We took up creating some treatment plants at some of the lakes. We made efforts to protect the smaller lakes, which were in the Master Plan. The BDA had taken up most of the government land earlier while developing the layout and some of the lakes were also covered. But I did not do that during my tenure. We wanted to protect the environment. Even in new layout, we had planned garbage segregation. What we had planned in BBMP area, the disposal is also required in BDA areas. Recycling of waste locally is also required. We also involved the Residents Welfare Associations. In the new layout, the BDA did good work. BDA also shouldered the responsibility of restoration of lakes. It helped in preserving the ecology and environment in the city.

□

Development with Human Touch

Like other states' Development Authorities, the main task of the Bangalore Development Authority (BDA), which I took over as Commissioner in June 2010, is to formulate plans for integrated development of the city. Any development plan involves provisions for civic amenity sites earmarked for different purposes. There are more than 100 purposes for which the civic sites are provided. These purposes include health, education, recreation, community facilities, playgrounds, roads, public gardens, parking, etc. That is why whichever part of the city has been laid out by BDA in the metropolitan city, good development has taken place. Good health and educational institutions, both in government and private sectors, have come up in those areas. Sites have also been provided for police stations, community halls, market, etc.

Signal-Free Outer Ring Road

BDA develops the infrastructure for the city. During my tenure, we took up the projects for building a number of flyovers on the outer ring road, which is one of the major roads in the city. Starting from Silk Board and passing through Mysore Road Junction, it reconnects Silk Board. Between Mysore Road and Silk Board, via Hebbal, more than 15 flyovers were planned and successfully completed. I personally monitored the progress of those flyovers on a monthly basis. As a result, the road became signal free in real sense. We also identified ten other major arterial roads and made them signal free for seamless movement of traffic.

Low-Cost Flats for the Deprived

Building of houses was a turning point in the history of BDA. Earlier, it mainly focused on allotting sites, which were in huge demand. These sites were bought mainly for resale, hoarding or for investment purpose. In that situation, the economically deprived sections of people did not get any site or house because of their low paying capacity. I proposed to build houses for the low-income group people wherever the BDA or government lands were available. Firstly, we conducted a survey to ascertain the number of such families, and then searched locations where BDA land was available and also took some land from the state government. Then amalgamating all those sites, we converted that entire land into a housing scheme for the economically deprived. Under the scheme, we built only one and two-bedroom multi-story flats, introducing new technology in construction. Major complexes came up near Kengeri and in some other areas. People watched the good quality construction that we ensured. That is why when we invited applications for the flats, the demand was so high that we were unable to meet all the applications. Since we counted only construction cost, and not the cost of the land, the flats were very cheap. Many people living on rent shifted there instantly. This single project alone changed the reputation of the BDA in the field of building houses. This initiative was highly appreciated. It helped the economically deprived people in a big way. We had planned more than 5,000 houses in a year and the total target was to build 30,000 houses. During my tenure 5,000 houses were built.

Alternative Sites to Land Losers

Another major discrepancy that I noticed was about a large number of people whose land was acquired, but they did not get the alternative sites. The BDA acquired their lands, allotted those lands to others, but did not grant alternative sites to them. As per the policy, the sites for them have to be kept aside and only the remaining land is marketed. But here, the officials notified and allotted all the land to public without ensuring sites for them. The farmers, who lost their land, frequently visited the BDA office with their complaints. It was really a pathetic situation. Their land was taken and given away to someone else and they became landless. I took up their case and allotted them sites wherever they were available. The number of such people was about 1,000. They were very happy and tearful when they got the possession of the sites. They said their problems were addressed for the first time and they were actually heard by the Administration. This is how we introduced a human touch in the BDA functioning.

We also cleared the old pending issues like small measurement differences, etc. We ensured that such cases are attended and resolved on fast track. We also removed the middlemen by installing CCTV cameras and restricting the entry of unauthorised persons in the office. We tried to ensure transparency in the whole system.

Resolution of Arkavathy Controversy

The Arkavathy Layout controversy in Bangalore brought a bad name to the BDA. About 8,000 people were given sites. Since there were people who had lost land, we gave them the top priority. We addressed the problems of the farmers. There were demands for denotification, but we did not agree to them. But I think the same intensity of addressing the issues did not continue later.

Kempe Gowda Layout was one of the four Layouts, which were planned for larger area. There were also some issues related to land acquisition. We gave the market price to the farmers and they granted their consent. I got government approval for it. Now acquisition of land is very difficult in BDA. It can no more construct houses. So, we have shifted our focus from acquiring land and allotting it to people to building multi story flats. It caters to the needs of large numbers of people. Anybody comes to buy sites even on loan. But in housing, it is mostly those who really need a house opt for it.

Land Audit

One of the major problems with the BDA was its assets that it acquired or allotted from time to time. There was no proper land audit telling how much land was acquired, how much was developed, how much was sold and how much was given to whom and how. Therefore, we got the entire area, which was notified and acquired by the BDA, surveyed. A database was prepared electronically. It basically helped us to identify the encroached sites and other areas, which were not then in the BDA possession. Then we started action for the removal of the encroachment. The property freed from encroachment was huge. At some places the construction had been started, while some sites were unbuilt. However, we could not free the whole encroachment. It is basically a constant exercise. In fact, that freed land gave us maximum revenue that year. When the land had been acquired, its value was very less, but by that time it was much more. Therefore, even if we recovered a small area, we got huge revenue on its auction. It is now the major source of revenue for the BDA. Thousands of acres of land fall in this category.

Thwarting Political Patronage to Encroachers

Removing encroachment is not an easy task. There is huge resistance not only from the encroachers but also from the political leaders of those areas. Litigation in court is also there. There are some vested interests too. For example, private developers and builders who buy such land or indirectly have agreements with the landholders; they even fund the encroachers to litigate against the BDA. This struggle constantly goes on. The land is a major issue in city areas because of its high value. We have to work in a very complex situation. We also have to seek police help at times, and taking their help is not an easy task in most of the cases. Though there is one SP in the BDA, he too has to depend upon others for help. Removing encroachment is akin to a war like situation. You have to make all the preparations and keep everything secret and strike suddenly maintaining an element of surprise. In such activities, one undergoes enormous pressure. Some people even approach the Chief Minister or other senior ministers and leaders directly.

The allotment of discretionary sites too is a big challenge. MLAs and other people regularly come for allotment or exchange of the sites. Sometimes the officers in the BDA leak information, which further complicates the problem. Pressure is there, but you have to uphold the rules and regulations.

The overall experience of BDA was very good. But that job does not have that much pressure as was in the BBMP.

□

UNDERSTANDING HEALTH OF THE SOIL

Despite increased use of fertilisers, the declining productivity in the farms has been worrying the farmers all over the country. Soil testing is, undoubtedly, the best scientific tool to assess the inherent power of the soil, but most farmers have been ignorant of it and they depend upon the fertiliser dealers for advice. The Soil Health Card Scheme launched by the Centre in February 2015 is being seen as a good beginning.

Soil testing was initiated in India in the beginning of planning era by setting up of 16 laboratories in 1955. The soil health studies review the complete health of the soil right from its functional characteristics to water and nutrient contents and other biological properties. It also provides corrective measures that a farmer can adopt to obtain a better yield. Andhra Pradesh has taken the lead in distribution of Soil Health Cards. Tamil Nadu, Punjab, Uttar Pradesh, Chhattisgarh, Telangana and Odisha have also displayed good interest. However, the response in some states like Haryana, Kerala, Mizoram, Arunachal Pradesh, Sikkim, Tamil Nadu, Goa, Gujarat, Uttarakhand and West Bengal has been sluggish. The government has set the target of issuing soil health cards to all farmers by the year 2016-17. In order to create a single national database on soil health, the Government has engaged the farmers through a web portal. Increase in productivity will eradicate the poverty of farmers, and productivity and production cannot be improved until the quality of land improves. Soil Health Card can prove to be a revolutionary step in farming sector of India.

Farming Becomes Profitable

Principal Secretary, Department of Agriculture from June 2012 to January 2013

Agriculture is, undoubtedly, the mainstay of Indian economy. But the problems faced by the farmers are never ending. It is because the agriculture in our country is still a gamble—heavily dependent upon rains and monsoon activity. Agriculture as a profession is not new to me. I come from an agriculturist family and I have actively worked with my father in the field during my school days. Even while serving, whenever I went home, I joined the farming activities.

Buffer Stock of Agricultural Produce

However, working in the Department of Agriculture as Principal Secretary from June 2012 was a different experience. There are a large number of schemes for agriculture and the farmers. Some schemes are centrally sponsored like Rashtriya Krishi Vikas Yojna (RKVY), while some are state sponsored like International Crops Research Institute for the Semi-Arid Tropics (ICRISAT)'s Bhuchetana, etc. With the help of ICRISAT, schemes were launched for increasing the productivity of soil. The prime issue that we face in the Department of Agriculture pertains to the supply of agriculture inputs—seeds, fertilisers, etc which are to be provided to the farmers in time. Once there is rainfall, they immediately resume farming and at that very moment everything should be available to them. So, it has to be properly stocked. For it, we introduced the system of buffer stock of all the inputs. We supported the government agencies providing fertilisers and seeds and, through timely action, ensured that there is no problem in supplying these inputs.

Farm Equipments on Hire

Since equipment is very much vital for modern farming, we introduced the system of providing equipments on hiring basis. We started Customer Hire Centres where the agricultural equipments are stored at Hobli or talukas and they are provided to the farmers on a hire basis. Normally, the agricultural equipments are used by the farmers only during the operations and afterwards they lie idle. It is wastage of money for small farmers. Even then those who want to purchase the equipments are provided subsidy. The Customer Hire Centres helped all types of farmers whether small, big or marginal to get equipments on nominal rent. Dharmsthala Trust of Karnataka adopted several districts under this scheme. It was one of the very popular experiments initiated by the Department of Agriculture.

Soil Sampling

Another experiment was for testing the soils of all the farmers and then creating a soil data base. Earlier, the samples used to be collected on village basis, mostly one or two samples from each village. But at that time, we decided to take samples from every farmer's land. We did it by inviting tenders from the private agencies. We feel treating the soil is like treating the human beings. If the quality of soil is not good or the farmer does not know what his/ her soil requires, applying fertilisers mindlessly without knowing the requirement is of no use. It is like giving different medicines to a patient suffering from tuberculosis. Hence, proper education of farmers about the health of their soil is absolutely must. That is why we took up the task of soil sampling and testing in a big way. We have laboratories at districts level, but they did not have the wherewithal to examine the estimated 30 lakh soil samples. Therefore, we decided to engage private agencies too.

From Lab to Land

It needs no elaboration that all officers working in a department do not have the same level of commitment. Some are very slack in their approach, while some are not good in terms of public dealing. The same thing happened in the Department of Agriculture also. Secondly, there was also a disconnect between the Agricultural Universities and the farmers or a gap from lab to land. The laboratories conduct several experiments but their inventions or findings are not adopted on the ground by the farmers. There are indeed some best practices in many agricultural universities, but they are needed to be scaled-up and the information disseminated to the farmers. In that process, we normally lose out because of the existent gap between the lab and the land.

New Method of Selecting the VCs

We also introduced some best practices in selection of the Vice Chancellors (VCs) of Agricultural Universities. The posts of Vice Chancellors were never advertised then. We started advertising the posts. Earlier, the Universities used to collect applications from some people and select and appoint one of them. We stopped that practice and advertised it on papers. It was for the first time that advertisements were issued for inviting applications for the posts of VCs so that whoever is eligible can apply. Then a committee selected the most suitable candidate from those applications. I followed that practice in the Department of Higher Education too. We also reduced the number of syndicate members to make it more effective. Earlier, the non-official members unduly interfered in the decision-making process.

Education for High Yields

I tried to introduce a lots of reforms, but that was not to my satisfaction. Agriculture is a vast sector, which really needs lot of attention, because we give huge subsidies to this sector and so many people are engaged and dependent on it. Despite all efforts, the productively level is still not that good. There is huge difference in the productivity level if we compare it to other countries like Israel, China, etc. In Israel, the water efficiency is the best. But here we misuse or over use the water. As a result, the soil becomes alkaline and again the farmers request for treatment. One has to again invest money on its treatment. But then again they indulge in water intensive crops like sugarcane, etc. Lot of soil is getting decayed due to such ignorance in our country. The problem with the Indian farmers is that they do not learn a lesson from one mistake.

The soil health is very important and it has to be treated like human beings. So, symptoms have to be checked and what is required must be done. The people in the areas rich in agriculture, who indulge in water intensive crops, need to be educated so that they take up crops that yield more revenue. We have seen that rather than doing the traditional crops, people in areas like Mandya, some parts of Mysore, Hasan, etc do flood irrigation to grow paddy and sugarcane. They find it easy. But that does not give the maximum yield. Whereas fruit and horticulture crops yield more revenue in those areas. This type of education is required all over the state. We tried to initiate those actions, but the result was not satisfactory. It is not easy to change the mindset of farmers. They have their own preconceived notions. They don't take risks easily by opting for new areas unless they are sure that something is going to help them.

Suvarna Krishi Hondas

The major scheme that we introduced after lot of discussion was Krishi Bhagya. The idea was to capture rain water, pool it at one place and then put a plastic lining so that the water does not percolate. That water is available when rainfall is less during the rainy season. If there is a dry spell, they can use it then. Subsequently, once it fills up again, they can use it again during the second crop. The experiment not only recharges and rejuvenates the ground water table, but also mitigates the drought situations. It provides water to people and animals during drought-like situations and improves farmers' economic conditions by encouraging agricultural productivity. Apart from creating Suvarna Krishi Honda, there was also a provision for giving diesel pump sets. If an electric motor pump is required, we give that also. If they want solar pump, that can also be arranged. We have made all arrangements so that the farmers have water and pumping arrangements, and they use it through sprinklers or other methods of efficient water use. We got lakhs of applications from different districts. We had earmarked ₹ 500 crore in the budget for it. However, the response in the first year was sluggish, but from the second year onwards, there is huge rush at Krishi Hondas.

We took effective steps to curb farmers' suicide by rationalising bank loans. During my posting in Department of Agriculture I visited Kenya to study the agriculture patterns there. After studying their patterns, I happened to see a wildlife park, which was very interesting. Kenya is one of the best places where one can see the wildlife. In our country, we go on seeing animals that are in the cage and we move freely. But in Kenya, animals are free and the person seeing them is in the cage.

□

HOW TO MAKE FARMING LUCRATIVE

All innovations and technologies in the farm sector are of no use until they are not accepted and adopted by the farmers. Convincing them for it is the toughest task, because they don't change their age-old practices so easily. However, Krishi Vigyan Kendras (KVKs) have been developed by Agriculture Universities in most districts as these institutes transfer the technology from universities' labs to farmers' fields, this mechanism could not change the farmers' mindset to a great extent. Most farmers have small holdings. They lack information on the global supply-and-demand conditions that affect local prices; they have limited access to crop management know-how, and weather forecasts that impact agricultural operations. Access to such information could help transform their low-yielding plots to highly productive farms.

The Government of India has set the target of doubling farmers' income by 2022 by focusing on not only the agriculture but also the allied sectors like poultry, fishery and dairy. It is believed that a family can save up to ₹ 3 lakh a year by doing the integrated farming. Prime Minister in March 2016 launched a 'Kisan Suvidha' app, which aims at providing information to farmers on weather, market prices, farm machinery as well as identification and management of crop pests and diseases. Another app 'Pusa Krishi' was launched on July 12, 2016 to provide farmers with the information related to new varieties of crops, resource conserving cultivation practices as well as farm machinery, and implements will help in increasing returns to farmers. Collective efforts are needed on the part of the scientists, government machinery and the opinion leaders to motivate farmers to adopt new technologies as they can help them make farming profitable.

Ensuring Innovations from Lab to Land

I was in the Department of Urban Development for about two and a half months. Then I was posted back, and I opted for Agriculture only in March 2013. Since many interests remain active in the Department of Urban Development, I was not found to be a convenient person for those interests to achieve their agenda. The officers working below me also appeared uncomfortable. I took one officer to task. I told him on his face that he would have to face the legal consequences and suffer. I think that person went ahead and told the powers that be. And they immediately took the decision to shift me. I had made my point of view clear in Arkavathy and other cases, whereas they wanted a different decision on my part, which I plainly declined. In Administration, it happens many times and that you have to put your foot down and clearly tell what is possible and what is not. If possible, you can do it within the frame of law. And if it is not we are not there to do that. But, unfortunately, in the present system there are people willing to do anything. And, people in power, look for such people. They want the convenient and not the inconvenient ones.

Uncompromising Inning

Fortunately or unfortunately, my reputation has been of an officer who travels faster, very strict, rule minded, does not listen to wrong things, etc. Many people don't like that. In a case of Cauvery Nigam (I was told by somebody) when they told the Minister that Mr. Meena is an honest and good officer, why have you transferred him". His immediate reaction, while laughing, was "his goodness is of no use for me". It means the goodness has no value for them. Their only concern is how their interests are served. That is the general tendency nowadays. That is why the Administration has deteriorated. If the officers and the people who make the law decide not to follow the law, there is no way to implement the law. Law can be distorted or interpreted in any way, if both sides join hands. There are three pillars in governance—Legislature, Executive and Judiciary. If one of them is not there the system will collapse. That is what, unfortunately, happened in the Department of Urban Development. Nowadays healthy balance is getting unbalanced. I never thought of getting any particular posting. I happily reached wherever I was posted.

Promoting Agriculture Practices through SHGs

I opted to come back in the Department of Agriculture, because I thought I should spend more time in this department. Immediately upon returning, I again started visiting all Agriculture Universities. I went to every district, held interactions with officers, reviewed actions taken on earlier schemes like Krishi Bhagya, Bhoochetna, etc. I also interacted with the Self-Help Groups, which are very strong in rural areas and some are really doing good work. I decided to utilise that strength for propagating water conservation, modern agriculture practices and telling about the government schemes. The problem in our system is that schemes are formulated with noble objectives, but they are not properly delivered. Because either the officer is not interested or parties with vested interests want to draw unfair advantage from that, or there is ignorance about the schemes among the people. That is how the delivery fails. Money is spent with good intention, but the actual benefit is not derived by the intended beneficiaries. This is the bane of today's system.

This can be plugged if we really take people together, involve them in the system and act with transparency. But this happens only in theory, not in practice. Take the example of Agriculture Universities. There are four Agriculture Universities and hundreds of Krishi Vigyan Kendras where the Government of India, state government and the universities spend huge sums of money. But the connection between the farmers and Krishi Vigyan Kendras is poor. Most of the research done in the labs do not reach the farmers' fields. If something is useful it should reach the farmers quickly and the farmers should be educated to adopt it.

Creating Models

Practically, most of our agriculture scientists do not go to the fields to educate the farmers about which crop should be grown when, what are its advantages, how can they increase productivity, etc. If they demonstrate it in some fields it leaves huge impact. Out of 30,000 villages, if we demonstrate it in 10,000 fields too, the impact will be huge. We went to a village in Belgaum where people use only organic fertilisers made of cow dung or green manure. They do not use chemical fertilisers at all. Last year, there was drought like situation in that area, but the moisture in their fields was more compared to the fields where chemical fertilisers are used. With only a little rainfall, they had a good crop. People from other villages regularly visited that village to see how it all happened. We need to create such examples involving the farmers.

Promotion of Organic Farming

Impressed with this experiment, we decided to have at least 100 acres of land in each revenue Hobli (taluk) for promoting organic farming. We wanted to have that much area in all 700 Hoblis on annual basis. So, we created lots of organic farmers' groups. Now they are growing and marketing organic products on a large scale. If they market it in an integrated way, there is a huge market for organic products. Certification, monitoring and education are to be done. That is what we successfully did in the second term.

Farmer Producer Organisations

In horticulture, we promoted Farmer Producer Organisations (FPOs)—a kind of company, which takes the products from the farmers, markets them and ensures a good return to them. We worked on creating more than 100 such FPOs. We hired some motivators also for it. The experiment had a very good impact.

'Krishi Mela' a Big Hit

Then we developed Vegetable Producer Clusters around Bangalore. That too was a big hit. We were also a leading state in implementation of Rashtriya Krishi Vikas Yojana (RKVY). Stressing on research, we told the Agricultural Universities to focus on developing new varieties of crops. Then Krishi Melas were popularised. The Mela organised in Dharwar University attracted more than 10 lakh farmers. Farmers came with eatables with them in the morning and went back in the evening with a renewed vigour. Some stayed at night too, so that they could learn something on the next day too. Most of them took keen interest in seeing the new technology. Some Universities now hold such Melas in every district. In Bangalore, we also organised an international conference of farmers to share the best practices of our Agriculture Universities.

Any breakthrough in agricultural research or technology is of no use if it is not adopted by the farmers. Surely, to convince the farmers for it is the toughest job, because most farmers don't change their age old practices so easily. But this is also a tried and tested fact that adoption of innovations help transform the low-yielding fields to highly productive farms. It is the collectively responsibility of the Krishi Vigyan Kendras, opinion leaders, etc to motivate farmers to adopt the new farming technology and also keep them updated about all aspects from recent technology to market prices.

□

Unlocking the Potential of Growth

Principal Secretary, Department of Urban Development from January 2013 to March 2013

Armed with the extensive experience of BBMP, BDA and also as Deputy Commissioner for preparing Master Plan, I set some priorities soon after joining the Department of Urban Development as Principal Secretary in January 2013. I was in this Department only from January 2, 2013 to March 12, 2013, and the top priority for me was to prepare Master Plans for all urban bodies keeping in view their future needs of at least next two decades.

Road Development in Master Plan

Preparing and following the Master Plan is the right way of developing a city. What should come in which area has to be thought, discussed and assessed depending upon the potential of the area. The Master Planner has also to visualise how to trigger the growth. I give a simple example. The land value in an inaccessible area is generally very less. The day you announce building a road there, its value jumps 10 times immediately. It happens only with the very idea of road, even before building the road. The day the Road is built the value goes up 100 times. You can see the example of Outer Ring Road in Bangalore. So much development has taken place around that road. That is the way where people can move faster. It shows how important is road development in the Master Plan.

Similar is the case of development around lakes. If you follow proper development plan, the green space around the lake adds value to the development around it. This is possible in Master Planning. Hence, planning signal-free roads, civic amenities, what must be developed on which side are all technical things. That does not happen in our system today. That is why I wanted to do that.

Synergy in Different Agencies

Then translating the Master Plan into action is another important point. If the road exists, even if it is earthen only, the access and approach to that area unlocks potential of growth there. That is what the Master Plan does. We wanted to do it for all the cities. We were planning for vertical growth. Now it is horizontal growth by way of sites, etc. Private builders develop sites totally ignoring the development of infrastructure. They sell the sites and vanish. There is no water, electricity, road, etc. That is how poor development happens. We wanted to curb all those things. We had also planned to solve the traffic problem in Bangalore by preparing a grid system. I wanted to complete the Ring Road that I had planned when I was in the BBMP. I wanted to make an elevated road East, West, North, South connecting the Ring Road inside the city so that it gives a thorough fare. People take that road and easily pass through.

We also wanted to do lake development in a big way. Because of my earlier experience, I planned to maintain good synergy with other departments. Urban Development, Water Board, Town Planning, BDA, BBMP, etc. all should have synergy in planning and execution. Before an agency prepares the Road, all other Departments should finish their work and they should not damage the road after it is finished. It is the discipline, which has to be maintained in urban development. We also wanted to map the entire underground system on computer so that one knows which line exists where.

No Change in Land Use

The traffic problem in Bangalore is a major issue. It requires both concerted efforts and huge investment. The government does not give that much money. So, we wanted to adopt the PPP model. Under the JNNURM, we get some funds. We wanted to use those funds for city development. Another problem in Urban Development was the issue of notification. You could very well make a Master Plan. But people continue to request for change in land use. In the plan, it is shown for residential purpose, but some people want to use that for commercial purposes. If it is commercial in the plan, they want it to be changed into industrial. If it is industrial, they want it to be changed to commercial or residential. This is what happens when the actual development takes place. That is a continuous problem in urban development. The word 'denotification' gets so much bad publicity during that time. So, I focused on it too.

In Arkavathy area, we had several issues. Lot of litigation was there. People were approaching for leaving the land. Lot of pressure was there on me, but I refused. I plainly said we cannot denotify or vacate any area. When I was on leave, some people in the Department tried to change the schemes. But I refused to budge. I warned the officials also, if they did anything illegal, they would have to face the legal consequences and I would not be party to that. My style of functioning was not liked then. Then they decided that I should move out of the Department. But I was firm on doing nothing wrong.

Being Ahead of Development

Urban Development is a happening sector. You have to plan in the Department for future. The plan has to be conceived and then the development has to follow. The cities are growing because of migration of people because of job opportunities, better life style and facilities. But the infrastructure is not keeping pace with the development. The planners in cities of other countries plan for 50 or hundred years. That is why as the city grows, infrastructure takes care of those needs. But that does not happen in the urban areas of our cities. The problems are there in every city. Bigger cities have Master Plan, but the smaller cities do not have at all. There are seven Corporation areas in Karnataka where there are Master Plans and urban development authorities. But there the activities are very less.

By and large, urban development is a challenging sector and it's not easy to plan in a regular manner. It is really a big exercise. We need to plan for 50 years. You should always be ahead of development. Keep a watch which area is growing. If the area is growing, more population moves there only. Then you have to provide water, sewage, roads, etc in that area. A new airport has come up in Bangalore. Naturally, the growth is bound to happen around that. If there is only one road, it gets congested. If you have three-four approach roads, people can take any of them. If there is only one road, they will have to use that only. That is what is happening in Hebbal today. Everything is getting congested. This has to be planned and thought simultaneously.

□

THE DREAM OF EDUCATION FOR ALL

Despite enacting multiple laws, India is still to ensure education for all. Forget smart classrooms in every school, there is an acute shortage of teachers, blackboards and even school buildings. Over a lakh schools do not have a single blackboard and thousands of government schools operate without buildings. In a remote village in Arunachal Pradesh, there are more than 300 students in class X, which makes nearly 100 students in each classroom. Even in the National Capital Territory of Delhi, there are about 175 children in one classroom. "There is huge dearth of classrooms in government schools and there are schools where over 150 children study in one room. There is a school in north-east Delhi where 174 children are made to sit in one room," Delhi's Education Minister Manish Sisodia was reported saying on March 17, 2016.

Despite the enactment of Right to Education law in 2009, over 640 million children or more than a third of 6-14 year olds, continue to pay for their education. Every village is not provided with a school, which means the students have to go to other villages for education. Owing to this, parents usually do not send their daughters to school. About 1,05,630 schools in the country are run by not more than one teacher. In Bihar, as stated by the government in Assembly on April 1, 2016, a total of 5,871 primary schools did not have buildings. The condition is no different in other states. How the condition can be improved is a major challenge not only before the Administration but for the entire society.

Smart Initiatives for Smart Generations

Principal Secretary, Higher Education, from January 2015. Promoted as Additional Chief Secretary on October 22, 2015

The Higher Education Department of Government of Karnataka, which I joined as Principal Secretary in January 2015, manages more than 3000 colleges, over 50 universities, about 20 lakh students studying there and a large number of staff. The state has been a pioneer in the field of higher education for decades, but now the challenges have increased manifold. Hence, managing the affairs in such a big department is not an easy task. Introduction of the best practices in these institutions and further motivating them to conduct new experiments was an uphill task. Wider use of Information and Communication Technology (ICT) was found to be the best solution to most of the problems. Earlier, the ICT was used only in a few institutions and that too at minimal level.

Online Monitoring of Office Procedures

With the help of National Informatics Centre (NIC), we listed almost 85 initiatives wherein software modules were to be developed and implemented. All those modules were interconnected. They were not stand alone. They collectively formed one software. First, we introduced improvements in office procedures itself—how the files are kept, how the files are maintained, how the offices are audited by external agencies, what are the audit observations, monitoring of those audit observations, court cases of different institutions, who is following them on behalf of the Department, what is the status of the cases, etc. Secondly, decisions are taken in the Department at various levels and minutes are recorded. But what happens after the meeting was difficult to find—who followed those meetings and what were the actionable points, etc. We also decided to go online for these activities. So, we made a software for it known as 'paperless office suite'. It provided solution to all these problems. This can be replicated by every institution—college, university, offices, secretariat, etc. It has already been implemented at various levels including the offices, universities, secretariat, commissioner office, Directorate of Technical Education, higher education council, colleges, etc. Through this system, files can be monitored online and pendency can be reviewed at various levels. It is available for all government and private universities to adopt.

Software for Academic Activities

Thereafter, we got other softwares prepared, which basically pertained to academic part. We prepared an exclusive software for online admission in UG, PG, Polytechnic and other professional courses. It was introduced in all universities and colleges. Now the whole data of the students is electronically available. They now apply only one time. Depending upon the merit, reservation quota, etc., they get offers for admission from different institutions.

Monitoring of Students' Attendance

We also got a software prepared for monitoring the students' attendance. It enabled the teachers to see the names of the students on the screen itself and mark attendance by using a simple smart phone or any other gadget. We also prepared a class matrix—on which date who will take which period. The teacher goes on his date, opens the folder, students' names appear under the classroom heading, and he marks the attendance of the students. Once he submits the attendance, it goes to the central server, which immediately starts sending that information to the parents. If the child is absent in any class, the parents get the information through SMS or email. This not only provides feedback to the parents about their wards, but also makes the students more accountable.

Biometric Attendance

Since the poor attendance of the staff in the institutions was a big challenge, the ICT provided solution to that also. We introduced biometric attendance in all the colleges and offices. When the staff comes that logs in and when goes that logs out. For taking students' attendance the teacher has to be present. There too his presence is marked. We have advised all the private and grant-in-aid colleges also to adopt this software.

Content Sharing

This is a fact that the institutions work in their own environment. How the teacher is teaching in one institution is not known to the students and teachers in other institutions. Recording of the video lecture or other content, their preparations for the lecture, etc. are not available to other institutions. We requested the top-ranking institutions to share their contents with the government institutions. To our surprise, all of them readily agreed to share whatever they had, because it was for common good. We made a software for it and uploaded all those videos there segregating them class wise and chapter wise. The students could view any video of any institution relevant to his/her subject. It is like a You Tube search. We continued to add more and more video content in the software to help the students. We planned to deliver the whole content at the students' door step. If one has missed any class, one can see the video of that class anytime. We have already made available thousands of hours of content. Students and teachers in rural areas hugely get benefited from it. They can see how others are studying or teaching, which is not available to them.

Faster Degree Delivery

Other problematic area that we found was examination—conduct of exams, evaluation of answer sheets, preparing marksheets, result declaration, etc. These activities were taking a lot of time. With the help of NIC we prepared a common software for all the Universities. It is customised according to their parameters. As soon the student submits the answer sheets in examination, they are scanned and saved in the server. The scanned copy is then sent to the evaluator, who gives marks and enters them in the system. Then the system generates the marksheet and overall result for the student. That is what we implemented in all the Universities. The system is being validated by various universities. This is another revolutionary step. It is foolproof and nobody can tamper. This reduced the evaluation time and result declaration became faster. With the help of this software we can also get the copies evaluated by professors of other universities sitting anywhere. It was introduced from the academic session 2015-16.

Another major initiative is connectivity. We established reliable connectivity between the government universities, private universities, deemed universities, colleges, Grant-in-Aid colleges and students. The things, which were working standalone now have been brought together and are more interactive. Now, they can view the classes elsewhere, join video conferencing, data sharing, and communicate with others. It is yielding good results.

Electronic Question Bank

In addition to all these aspects, we prepared an electronic question bank. The question papers of all subjects and universities have been fed on a computer. Now the students can download the questions unit-wise and answer them using their mobile phones. Then the system evaluates the answers. It is an endeavour to make the internal evaluation more transparent.

Teacher-Student Exchange

Another initiative is teacher students exchange programme. Under this programme, we want the better institutions go to these institutions, which are not so good, especially in rural areas. Then the teachers of those institutions go there, talk to the teachers and students, exchange their views and educate them. Similarly, the rural institutions should visit the top-class institutions on certain days. We have told the institutions to do hand holding and work out a programme for the entire year as to how they are going to operate. As part of it, the first MoU was signed in October 2015. A good university can go to two-three districts. It is the idea, which nobody had thought of. We want that the best things should be known to everybody. A student studying anywhere is the nation's asset. They have to be taught in the best way. They have right to receive good knowledge. If there are resource constraints, they can be overcome through this initiative. This is the basic idea behind the whole exercise. Once this gets strengthened, it will be implemented all over the state.

Sharing of Best Practices

Another initiative is to collect the best practices and implement them in other institutions. In March 2015, we organised a conference inviting the Vice Chancellors of all the Universities. We asked them to indicate the best five practices they follow. They made presentations before all the VCs. Then we compiled those practices and prepared a booklet. It was very good learning experience for all of them. It was done for the first time. Then we told the colleges also to compile their best practices. During the hand holding, these best practices also help the institutions to emulate in their areas.

Common Website for All Institutions

We also developed the system of Education Electronic Management Information System (EEMIS) under which all colleges can have one common website. Even if they have their own website, they can link that with this website. The students need not open all the websites for different information; they can view all the information at one place. A standard website has been designed by NIC and each institution has to create its own page there. This has already started and colleges are being linked to it. We are also linking the grant-in-aid colleges with it. It is available to all institutions free of cost. This is very useful from the students', parents' and management's point of view. Through it, we can also monitor the class matrix, which class is taking place where, the activities of the colleges, their strengths and weaknesses, their assets, activities of the teachers, video conferencing, etc.

Smart Classrooms

We are also working on smart classrooms to strengthen the two-way communication. If some students are absent and the teacher wants to address relevant issue, this can be done by using satellite communication. We are also going to connect our State Institutes of Rural Development to the institutions. This will increase the reach and utility of the institutions.

These are only a few examples I have cited. Many more things are happening. I am sure these initiatives will help Karnataka become a model state in the field of higher education and other states will learn from it. These initiatives were basically introduced within eight months after my coming to the Department of Higher Education.

Undoubtedly, it was not free from hurdles. Resistance to change is always there. We need to first mentally prepare the people for such tasks. 'How can it happen' was the immediate reaction of many of the institutions. They also cited so many constraints. But we prepared them and successfully introduced all the changes and achieved good results. Challenges come up as you do any good work. But we have to face them and move forward.

□

Affordable and Accessible Education to All

We initiated many schemes in the Department of Higher Education to improve the standard of education and to ensure quality education to the largest number of students. Gnansangama is one of the initiatives, which has contributed a lot to achieve this objective. Under the scheme, studios have been set up in almost all universities for development of e-content and multimedia based e-content. Some universities already had such studios. We upgraded them according to the changing needs.

Uniform Curriculum

The prime objective of setting up these studios is to standardise the content of all prescribed curricula and also to make it uniform for all the universities. We have also endeavoured to make the teaching methodology common for all the universities. We constituted committees in various universities to prepare the common and standardised content for all the universities and that content is being digitised and animated. That standard content is being made available to all the universities and institutions throughout the state—both the government and private.

The basic idea is that the standard of teaching should improve and the teachers should give maximum content to the students in that form which the new generation likes today. This is the basic idea behind setting up these studios. These are multipurpose studio. Apart from generating the new content, we can also amend the old content at any stage. Hence, the studios are used for recording as well as upgrading the skills of the teachers. In that way, we believe that by setting up these studios, we will be able to generate more e-content and also use multimedia more effectively for content development, transmission and delivery to the students throughout the state.

Launching Exclusive TV Channel

We have also planned to have a separate television channel where the content can be made available to the students 24x7. It may be web based or whatever technology is best to serve the purpose shall be used. We will also be sharing all the content and the developments in education department with all the institutions. That will happen in the times to come.

Online Affiliation

Another useful initiative is creating a system for online affiliation of colleges and the institutions. Out of the total 17 universities in the state, we have 14 affiliating universities under the Department of Higher Education. Every year the institutions are supposed to apply for renewal of affiliation. The Local Inquiry Committee (LIC) visits these institutions and then makes its recommendations. It is a continuing exercise. But here more transparency is required in the whole system. We decided to make provision for online updating of all the records of institutions. We developed a software for it. And all institutions now upload their details in that software. The local committee, as and when it visits the institutions, records its observations and recommendations online only. And those recommendations are uploaded on the spot only. Therefore, they do not need to submit the reports to anyone. That provision is available in the system. The institutions can also know what are the recommendations of the LIC. If they do not recommend re-affiliation, why have they not recommended. The institutions will be able to remove the shortcomings pointed out by the Committee. If the committee does not make favourable recommendations for grant of affiliation, the institutions can further proceed accordingly. This way we have made it a transparent procedure. We started implementing it from the year 2015 itself for the remaining part of the academic year. It is one of the best practices that we have adopted in Karnataka. I am sure the institutions will find it useful.

Students' Data Base

Another initiative that we have taken is to create student data base. Presently, the institutions keep and maintain the data with them. Then the Department of Higher Education also keeps the data with it for disbursement of scholarship, etc. There is no uniformity in the database at the two levels. Now we have interlinked the data of students starting from Secondary School Leaving Certificate (SSLC) level (all the digitised data is available with the SSC Board), PU level (available at the PU board), to the admission data, which we receive online, etc. So, the Department will source this data from one point. It will help in curbing the duplication of scholarships, etc. They will get the same information from everywhere. The students will not be able to claim double benefits. This way the things have become more transparent. This will also help the institutions to collect their fees and the students will be able to get scholarship under various schemes of the state government.

These initiatives are part of the 100 innovative steps that we have taken in the state to improve the standard of education. The Department of Higher Education has strived to make quality higher education affordable and accessible to all sections of the students. With a firm concern for overall development of the students, the Department has taken keen interest to see that students belonging to the most backward communities, women and rural students are not deprived of the accessibility to tertiary education.

□

Making Sure Fair Assessment

Everybody supports the view that examination should be independent, impartial, fair and free from any kind of fraud. As the technology is growing, the free and fair evaluation is becoming a challenge. Presently, the human interference in examination system is very high at all levels—setting question papers, printing of question papers, dispatching them to the designated examination centres, students appearing for exams, custody of the answer sheets, dispatching of the answer sheets to designated places, evaluation of the answer sheets, filling the marks in the proforma and then final declaration of the results. Lot of people are involved in this whole process. The weaknesses of human beings are exploited for various reasons, may be for some considerations or something else. That has to be tackled. It is a big challenge for all the institutions.

In Karnataka, we wanted to provide a complete solution for this problem. Hence, we got a software prepared through National Informatics Centre (NIC). They worked on it for several months. After development of the software, it was tested in the Universities. First, they stored the previous data of students in the software. Then the new data was fed. It proved to be a good success everywhere. First, we rolled it out in Tumkur University and then in Mangalore and Bangalore Universities.

Electronic Delivery of Question Papers

The very idea of the examination software and reforms

is to deliver question papers just half an hour earlier to the centres. They can download the copies of the question paper. Number of copies was also restricted so that they cannot Xerox them. The copies of the questions were allowed to be printed as per the number of students appearing in the exam. The electronic delivery of the question papers proved to be very helpful.

Then biometric attendance of the students appearing in the exam was introduced. As soon as the exam is over, the answer sheets are immediately sent to the examination centres set up at the district level, where all the answer sheets were scanned. Every alternate page of the answer sheet was bar-coded. Even if it is scanned randomly, then too it can be assembled through the barcode. Then the digital copy goes for evaluation and the original copy is permanently in the custody of the institution. The evaluator has model answers in the system to compare, if they feel necessary. Then he gives the marks in the system itself. Once he/she submits the marks in the system, nobody can change them.

Reducing Physical Appearance

The same answer sheets can be sent to the second person in case the previous evaluator has given very high or low marks to some students. We can decide which range is to be reevaluated. Like this, moderation can be done. Any copy can be selected randomly and the evaluation can be checked. Then the marks get entered in the system electronically from where the mark sheets are generated and the result is declared. The same data is available for post result activities—after the person has completed the course, if somebody wants to cross check the certificate or marks, they do not need to physically move around the university. This way we have given them hand to hand solution for everything. We feel it helped us in regulating a lot of irregularities. Who worked and when or who is working on the system is known to us. The system is used only by the people who have been assigned this job. No one else can access it. So, they use it with full responsibility. There are certain things, which they cannot change. For example, they cannot make any correction in the marks even if they want.

Transparency in Evaluation

Presently, they can do it in the system, as there is no foolproof system. Now the private agencies are supplying software and the data are in their server. Even if we have physically received a hard copy, what has been finally entered in the system by the typist, becomes the final thing. Many a times there is mismatch in what is written in the hard copy and what has been entered in the system against the student's name. These things are possible in the present system. Now only the evaluator whose ID has been loaded in the system can evaluate the answer sheets. We will not give all answer sheets to one person. Once he has evaluated five copies, then only he will be given next five copies and that too randomly, not in sequence. An evaluator can get the copies of any number of universities. He can do the evaluation sitting at his home too. If any student wants to see his copy, the scanned copy can be sent on his/her email id.

The Registrars, who are normally under a lot of tension and stress because of exams, feel relaxed. It is system driven. It arrests the mischief normally done on the part of human beings. The staff and the evaluators are trained to work as per the system. We have already introduced it and from the academic year 2016 it has been implemented in all the Universities in the state. I hope for good and hustle-free days ahead for the educational institutions, staff members and the students.

□

PROMOTING 'OUT OF THE BOX' VISION

The syllabus designed and followed by different educational institutions has been under scanner for long. In most cases it fails to keep pace with the rapid change in technology and needs of various sectors. Since the syllabus has its own limitation and cannot be revised every year, there is a need to keep the students updated with the changes taking place in the education sector and also in the industry where they are to be employed after completion of their studies. Of course, many experiments are being conducted in several institutions across the country. Some institutions focus more on interaction with the experts and achievers in the classrooms, while some stress on practical experiences by the students in different industries.

At a time when most youth are not habitual of reading daily newspapers, magazines, participating in debates, discussions, seminars, etc, providing them outside input other than the syllabus is beyond any debate. It not only promotes ideation and a vision to think out of the box among the youth, but also equips them with the knowledge about various vital issues including awareness about current topics, issues emerging in the society, challenges being faced by the nation or the state, international issues pertaining to environment, education, health, culture and many other aspects related to the human life. It gives something what is not found in the classroom or the textbooks. Learning from one's experience is something, which is time-tested. This ultimately makes the students good citizens possessing good values and upholding the rich values of the country.

Assembly for Innovation

Innovative idea or motivation can click anywhere. We the Indians, since time immemorial, believe 'let the noble thoughts come from everywhere'. Following the maxim, the Government of Karnataka recently issued an order directing all colleges and higher education institutions to start the practice of 'daily assembly'. It happens in all primary and high school level institutions, but at Pre University (PU) and higher education level it is not there. People—the students, faculty members and staff members—normally don't gather together, except during the annual function or any other big event organised in the institution once or twice a year.

Ensuring Outside Input

The students come to the institution to study certain subjects, and only those subjects are mostly discussed in the classrooms. Not much outside input reaches the students. There is very little number of students who read daily newspapers, magazines or participate in debates, discussions, seminars, etc. By and large, the bonding to the institution is less and the knowledge horizon of students limited. Now, we have listed and identified about 200 subjects, which are mostly of national, international, state or individual importance. We picked up 50 to 60 topics from them and circulated to the principals of various institutions. We have advised the institution heads to commence the assembly 20 minutes ahead of the college timing, so that it does not interfere with the daily schedule of the college/ institution. They are expected to take 20 minutes for this session.

Inculcating New Knowledge

Since the assembly is an informal initiative to impart new knowledge to the students as well as faculty members, we have advised the institutions to choose the speaker themselves. They can also make use of the students having good oratory skills. Such students can be told to prepare topics of their choice in advance. Teachers can also be told to specially prepare for it. They can also invite a resource person from outside to speak on any particular topic. There is no any rigid set of rules or guidelines. Sufficient flexibility is there. They can choose the subject of their choice, which they find relevant in that context.

Feeling Mentally Energised

Such assemblies have already begun all over the state. First, we introduced them in government run colleges and now the grant-in-aid institutions have also been covered. These are being conducted with a positive impact on both the students and teachers. They learn several new things through them. Many new ideas click and they feel mentally energised to pick up new initiatives. It has also created a positive energy in the system and the institution. Since the beginning, the students are seen to be more responsive. Now if the students do not have class on a particular day, they sit in the library and do something positive. Lot of activities have started in colleges. The practice has received tremendous applause from different quarters.

Arming with Practical Information

The topics covered in the assemblies are very important. They arm the students with very useful and practical information such as the knowledge of the fundamental rights, fundamental duties, and awareness about various current topics and issues emerging in the society, challenges being faced by the nation or the state, international issues pertaining to the environment, education, health, culture and many other aspects of the human life. It gives them something that is not found in the classroom or in the textbooks. After all, the textbooks and the classrooms too have their own limitations. Everything cannot be accommodated in the textbooks. Learning from one's experience is something, which is time tested and cannot be found in the classroom or the textbooks. One needs to think out of the box to get innovative idea. That is why this experiment has been applauded and no negative feedback has been received from anywhere. I feel if it continues for a year or so, impressive change will be visible among the students and the institutions. They would become more responsive to the society and the nation and above all to their individual lives. We are making them good citizens possessing good values and upholding the rich values of the country.

Imparting New Vision

It is not a traditional pray system normally happens in the schools. The endeavour is to give the college students and faculty members something new, which leads them to a new direction in their lives. Major part of it is based on the practical experiences of the individuals or organisations, who have achieved something innovative. The main thrust is to give them a new vision. It also provides an opportunity to the students to become good orators. After all, good oratory skills must be acquired. This is the place where the institutions can start bringing in positive changes. There is no fixed timing to start the assembly. We have just advised them to start before the commencement of their daily schedules. They can fix their own timing. The response received so far is very enthusiastic. At certain places, the students have opined that the time is not sufficient and more time should be provided for interaction. We have granted flexibility to the institutions to extend the time as per the requirement.

The experiment is highly beneficial and I feel it should begin in all the colleges whether public or private or even in the industries and enterprises. Motivation can come from anywhere. It is up to us how we catch and imbibe it in our lives.

□

BRIDGING THE SKILLS GAP

Despite the growing awakening for higher education among the parents and students and also the increasing growth in the number of higher education institutions, both in private and public sectors, India faces a significant skill gap. According to Aspiring Minds National Employability Report 2016, which is based on a study of more than 1,50,000 engineering students who graduated in 2015 from over 650 colleges, 80% of them are unemployable. In terms of cities, Delhi continues to produce the highest number of employable engineers, followed by Bengaluru and the western parts of the country. Kerala and Odisha entered the top 25 percentile list of most employable states, but the northern states like Punjab and Uttarakhand dropped to the 2nd and 3rd quartile. Another survey by Aspiring Minds across 500 engineering colleges and 30,000 students revealed in August 2015 that 97% of the engineering graduates cannot speak English required for jobs in corporate sales or business consulting. More than 51% engineering graduates are not employable based on their spoken English scores. More astonishingly, 61% engineers possess grammar skills no better than a Class 7 student.

All these indicate towards the need for an urgent upgradation in education and training system and also demand our attention towards bridging the rural urban divide in quality education. Definitely, the students with rural background lack exposure to technology and the overall matrix available to the students in urban areas. How to fill this gap is a challenge for the policymakers. The experts say Industry-Academia connect, hand-holding between the urban and rural institutions, students and faculty exchange and access to quality smart classes to all could prove to be a game changer in this regard.

Bridging the Rural-Urban Divide

The Rural-Urban divide in higher education has been nagging the minds of policymakers and educationists for a long time all over the country. Though several steps have been taken at various levels in different parts of the country to bridge this divide, the results are not yet satisfactory. We in Karnataka brought the private and public universities together to exchange their programmes and faculties and empower the students and teachers in rural areas. The initiative got the applause from various quarters.

Every Student Deserves Quality Education

It is generally observed everywhere in the country that the institutions work in their own independent environment. How the teachers teach in one institution is not known to the students or teachers in other institutions. Normally, the students in rural institutions are deprived of the good content due to various reasons. That is why they perform poorly compared to the students in urban areas. We decided to change this scenario because we firmly believe that quality education is every student's right.

Delivering e-content

We have around 3000 colleges and more than 50 universities catering to the needs of about 20 lakh students in the state. We requested the top ranking or A-grade autonomous institutions of the state to share their content with the government institutions. All of them happily agreed, as it was for common good. We immediately developed an exclusive software and also a matrix—class-wise, chapter-wise and subject wise. All the videos were uploaded in that portal. A student sitting anywhere can view any video which is relevant to his/her subject. It is like a 'YouTube' search. We still go on adding more and more videos to the portal. It is a government server produced by e-governance department. We are also prepared to deliver the e-content to the doorstep of the students so that they can access and study at any time. If any of them have missed any classes they can view that content also. We are going to do it in a big way. We have already collected thousands of videos.

Teacher-Student Exchange Programme

Compared to the urban areas, the students and teachers in rural areas have hugely benefited from this initiative. They can also see how others are teaching or studying, which was not available to them earlier. This is one of the best practices, which has been started in Karnataka.

Another major initiative that we have taken to bridge the rural urban divide is the teacher-student exchange programme. Under the programme, we want the better institutions to go to those institutions, which are in a poor condition due to various reasons especially in rural and remote areas. The teachers from such institutions go there, talk to those teachers, exchange views and educate them. Similarly, the students from rural areas visit these institutions on some fixed days. Encouraged over the initial results we have told them to do more handholding and work out a programme for entire year. As part of this, the first MoU was signed between PES University, Tumkur University and Kuvempu University on September 12, 2015. It has been named as 'TUPUKU'. The Higher Education Department has identified 12 private universities including the PES University, Dayanand Sagar University, MS Ramaiah University and Alliance University.

Promoting Handholding

They now go to three districts and work out how this handholding can work in different areas and different fields. It has already started. We are sending other universities also to other areas to conduct the same programme. We want that the best things should be known to everybody. For us any student studying anywhere is a nation's property. He/she has the right to be taught properly, the right to receive good knowledge and the right to learn better. If the resource constraints and problems exist, they can be overcome through such programmes. Their exposure can enhance their knowledge. This was the basic idea behind starting this activity. This will happen more all over the state in the time to come.

Sharing Best Practices

Another step that we have taken is exchange of the best practices followed in various universities or the institutions. In the month of March, 2015 we held a two-day conference inviting all the Vice Chancellors of state, deemed and public universities asking them to list their five best practices. They made presentations before all the Vice Chancellors. We compiled them in the form of a book. This has helped all the institutions in the state to adopt the best practices being followed in other institutions. It was for the first time that the best practices were exchanged at institutional level. Now we are going to tell the colleges also to exchange their best practices with each other. Similarly, we are also trying to encourage innovations at different levels.

□

ARRESTING WORKPLACE ABSENTEEISM

Reaching late in the morning, longer lunch hours and leaving the office early were common scenes in majority of the government offices till September 2014, when the Central Government made biometric attendance mandatory in all its offices. It worked magically as the rate of the staff reaching office in time and staying for longer hours increased substantially. Analysis of first three months i.e. September, October and November 2014 revealed that the average presence time of the staff in office rose by about 20 minutes per day. In terms of man-days with an average of 8.5 hours per working day, the gain was equivalent to an additional workforce of almost 1,900 employees every single day. The habitual absentees also now cannot mark their presence while remaining absent. As on November 28, 2016 a total of 2,00,775 employees were registered with 671 government organisations and the average time for the employees reaching office was 9.32 am.

Globally, 30 to 35% of the pay costs of companies are absence-related. Ten per cent of the payroll costs are linked to unplanned absence globally. In India, this cost is about 15 to 20%. If the cost leakage due to workforce mismanagement is 3 to 5% globally, in India it is three times that of the global numbers. A study by Assocham in 2010 had revealed the absenteeism rate as 20%. The resultant cost in terms of lost productivity, the study estimated, was 80 billion rupees. In police, tax collection, education, health, power, water supply—in nearly every routine service—there is rampant absenteeism, indifference, incompetence and corruption.

Class Bunk – No More an Issue

Students bunking classes is a common problem everywhere. Teachers and parents as well as policymakers are deeply worried over it for a long time. It is a serious issue because it is not limited to just running away from study; it leads to many social and ethical problems including the crimes.

Use of ICT is a Good Remedy

In the booming age of digital technology, the traditional methods are proving ineffective to curb this tendency. Therefore, we in Karnataka decided to use the information and communication technology (ICT) to check the menace. Our experiment proved to be a big hit in government institutions. Now grant-in-aid and private institutions are also going to adopt it. This method can be applied to schools also all over the country.

Monitoring Students' Attendance

After analysing the problem and involving the experts, we developed a software for monitoring the students' attendance. Through the software one can, only by using simple Smartphone or any other gadget, follow the students. Teachers can view attendance of the students on the screen itself. We have also made a class matrix determining who will take which period and on which date. The teacher can open the folder on that date and see the students in the classroom. He can, by calling the names of students, mark their presence or absence. He submits the information electronically to the Institution. Then the information goes to the central server, which immediately sends information to the parents. If a child is absent, the information goes to the parents through SMS or email informing them that their ward has not attended the class. Now, the parents are also aware of the movements of their wards and they can question them about their absence. Students are now more accountable. Their attendance is properly recorded.

Biometric Attendance

Since there have been complaints of teachers not teaching in the class, we introduced biometric attendance system for the teachers. When they come, they log in and when they go out they log out. The teacher's attendance is also marked when they take the students' attendance. Now we are going to introduce this system in all grant-in-aid and private colleges also. In this way the entire system is set to witness a lots of changes.

Higher Education Department in Karnataka caters to the needs of over 3000 colleges, over 50 universities and over 20 lakh students pursuing their studies all over the state. Karnataka has been a pioneer in the field of higher education. As the number of institutions and students grew, the challenges also grew. We made the best use of technology to not only manage the things but also to make the functioning more transparent.

Digitalising Office Procedure

We listed about 85 initiatives and developed software modules through the NIC. All the modules are interconnected. We began with improvement in the office procedures—how the files should be kept, how the record should be maintained, how they are audited by external agencies, what are the auditors' observations, monitoring of those observations, court cases, how many court cases are there in each institution, who is following them, what is their status, decisions taken and how they are followed at the implementation stage, what are the actionable points in the minutes, etc. Now all these are monitored online. We have named this software Paperless Office Suite, which has made things faster and more convenient. The model is very simple and can be replicated by every institution. It can be done at college, university, and office or secretariat level. Not only in the Secretariat, Directorate of Technical Education and Higher Education Council level but also in many other offices and Universities it has successfully been implemented. Now we are in the process of implementing it at the college level. Then it can be applied to schools too.

Online Admission

Now files are monitored online. Pendency can also be reviewed at different levels. The software is available to all government and private universities. We have also produced some software, which pertain to the academic part at college level. A software has been produced for online admissions for under graduate, post graduate, polytechnic and other professional courses. The data related to students is maintained electronically. The students need to apply only once. They are no longer required to apply separately in every institution.

The ICT has made things faster, cheaper and transparent. We should make the best use of it.

□

Skilling to Think Beyond the Box

Take up one idea. Make that idea your life—think of it, dream of it, live on that idea. Let the brain, muscles, nerves, every part of your body, be full of that idea, and just leave every other idea alone. This is the way to success."

—Swami Vivekananda

Skilling the students as per the changing needs is a major challenge everywhere. All governments, from Centre to States, are deeply worried over it and they are taking some or the other steps in this regard. Taking it in a serious way we, in Karnataka, have signed MoU with the National Skill Development Corporation (NSDC). We have also involved some private players in this task. The initial response is very encouraging.

Empowering with Extra Skills

We are going to impart extra skills to every student who wants to receive it. The students will get a certificate at the end of the course or after completing the required number of training hours. This certification will help them get employment in the area they are interested in. We have started it from January 2016. We have also received proposals from various other organisations and are going to involve them depending upon the interest shown by the industry. In coming years, we want to make Karnataka a talent pool for supply of manpower not only for Karnataka but also for the entire country and the rest of the world. So, we are giving more emphasis to the students who are in arts, science, engineering, or even in the professional courses where they do not get the desired employment.

Helping Improve Spoken English

In every college, we are also starting the facility to learn spoken English, as good spoken English has emerged as a basic requirement nowadays. It is more required by the rural students where there is not much emphasis on learning English. They have talent but because of poor command over spoken English they find it difficult to communicate despite knowing the subject well.

Promoting Academia-Industry Connect

For it, we are exploring the opportunities everywhere. We are putting the industry in our Board of Studies so that they can advise on what changes could be brought about in the curriculum. In the times to come, I think, lot of synergy will happen between the academia and the industry. The skills of both the students and the teachers will be upgraded to a large extent. We are using the ICT for this purpose to reach a large number of people simultaneously. Satellite communication is going to help us greatly in this task. The Skill development will take place along with their regular studies or they will learn after their study hours. We hope, in the days to come the students will get huge benefit out of it.

Exploring Original Ideas

My advice to all the students who are seeking jobs, or will seek in near future, is that those who have original ideas should start their own enterprise. If it's possible they should become entrepreneurs. That is also an option to excel in the life. Of course, going in other fields like private or government jobs is also left to you. Competitive exams and other options are also open. We also encourage students to prepare for competitive exams, especially the exams conducted by Union Public Service Commission (UPSC), Karnataka Public Service Commission (KPSC), banks, and railways, as they are major employers. We have placement offices. We are telling the institutions to take more interest in it and see that maximum students are get placed.

Success Requires Hard Work

The students who prepare for competitive exams should remember that success is not easy to come by. It requires serious efforts and hard work. There is no shortcut to hard work. Some genius said that for success it is 99% preparation and 1% inspiration. That is how it is. One can be inspired by certain people, stories or activities. But ultimately only inspiration is not enough. You have to make efforts. Set your target. One thing is sure, once you set your target high and make efforts which are within your means then you can leave the rest to fate. And most likely you will get success. It has been proven. Our students who are going to prepare for all these exams must have confidence. With self-confidence, they can succeed. That is my advice.

Focused Concentration

The last word is that focused concentration is absolutely necessary. You cannot have many things in mind—today one goal and tomorrow another. You have to set your goal and firmly believe in that. Once you do that make sincere efforts to make it possible. What makes the difference in studies is the concentration. Some people can recall after one serious study only, while some do not properly recall even after studying twice or thrice. Everyone has a different level of concentration. What makes a difference is focused concentration. That is important.

□

Believe in Yourself

The painful trend of suicides by some students in different parts of the country including Kota (Rajasthan) is highly disturbing. Not only the parents, educationists, sociologists but also the policymakers are deeply worried over it. I feel it is the outcome of unduly burdening the students with excessive expectations. Parents expect the best from them. They want their child to excel and be number one, which is not always possible, as every child has a different potential. Everyone cannot be number one. But majority of the parents do not accept this fact. Their unrealistic expectations exert undue pressure on the students, which ultimately develop excruciating stress in them and they fail to cope up with it.

You are the Best

It is a competitive world. Everybody's limitations, capabilities and strengths are different. When there is so much competition, how can every parent expects that his/her ward always stands number one, or among the top ten, top twenty, etc. The killer trend has deepened so much in the minds of the parents that they are not ready to accept the reality and continue to put a target before them disregarding their capabilities. At the same time they do not take care of the fear connected with not being able to achieve the target.

If the target is fixed in a positive sense, then it plays the role of real motivation to excel in life. The child should be told in clear terms that you try your best and if you fail this time then try again. Otherwise leave it, think of something else. There are many other options available nowadays. This is the type of attitude that should be developed and this much comfort level must be provided to the students.

Show Maturity

The students should also show some maturity. At the age of 20 plus they become mature enough. They should realise that they have to make sincere efforts in the competition. If you fail, it does not give you the right to end your life. Life is too precious. Another thing is that the life does not end at IITs, NITS, IIMs, Medical only. If you succeed, well and good, and if you fail, there are many other avenues also. The students should have that understanding too when they start preparing for any competitive examination. We see many people who fix a target of becoming only IAS and do not try any other avenue. My advice to such students to first pick up some employment and then try for whatever they want to be. It will reduce financial burden on the parents, generate self-confidence and make the students gain some experience in the life. But many times, many students commit this mistake and continue to depend upon their parents for a long time. That should also be avoided. (Children should learn the knack of opening of lock.) Some prepare well, but do not score well.

Never Feel Dejected

Some prepare all the time but even then they fail. We should take things as they come and always believe in ourselves. The self-confidence should never be shaken. No extreme steps should ever be taken by anyone. We must value life, which is the opportunity given by the Almighty only once. Instead of taking our own life, we should rather dedicate our life to other causes. If you have not succeeded in one area you may succeed in other area. Rather dedicate your life for promoting the cause, which you have not been able to fulfill. That option is also there for us. There are many people we have seen in our life who have successfully shown it. I know a person in Karnataka who could not pass even eighth standard but today owns more than 100 educational institutions so that none should be deprived of education. A number of leading scientists failed several times but it did not stop them from making repeated efforts. There are many successful people in the world who were not very good at studies but excelled perfectly in life. This type of desire and commitment can give a new direction to the life.

Counselling of Students

Undoubtedly, lots of things need to be changed in the education system also. The curricula have been designed keeping in mind the local needs. Now we should think with a global perspective. Our students should be prepared not only to work in India, but at the global level. The education system should dynamically be changed in such a way that we assimilate good ideas, good contents and the things, which are required to earn a good livelihood.

The educational institutions should also start helplines to address the stress developed among the students due to any reason. When a student is psychologically stressed, at that very moment he/she should be provided with proper counselling. Some voluntary organisations can also be engaged in this task. The coaching institutions, which impart training or coaching should have inbuilt mechanisms to address the stress of the students. The faculty members should also be sensitised in a manner that they motivate the students in a way that there are many other options if one fails in an endeavour. Parents should also motivate the students that they make your best and leave the rest to the Almighty. We have the right to do, but not the right to show the result. Nobody has control over the result. Therefore, don't bother about the results. Rather have the feeling that

I have done my best. Once you have that satisfaction, rest of the things will follow.

Hence, believe in yourself. You are braver than you think, more talented than you know, and capable of more than you imagine. Believe in your infinite potential. Your only limitations are those you set upon yourself. Don't doubt yourself, that's what haters are for. Don't pretend to be what you are not, instead, pretend to what you want to be, it is not pretence, it is a journey to self realisation.

□

Self-Confidence is the Key

Keeping in view the large number of rural students appearing for Civil Services and other competitive exams, the coaching centres operating mostly in urban areas should have a pan-India presence having centres even at the District and Block Headquarters. This will help the students get quality coaching and good revenue generation for the coaching centres.

Exploitation by Coaching Centres

For some time, the trend of preparing for Civil Services examinations is getting stronger. Despite advancements in the economy in diverse fields, lots of people have interest in the Civil Services, which is a good thing. To cater to their need coaching centres have been mushroomed. Lots of advertisements are seen in the newspapers about coaching centres. Many centres have come up in capital cities and even in smaller areas at District headquarters. Many of these are doing well, but most of them only have a commercial agenda in mind. They try to exploit the psyche of the students and their parents. Many people having good resources go there and spend money. Some get through, but most do not.

Practical Training to Rural Students

Most talented students from rural areas or weaker segments of the society do not get access to the best institutions. Some of them are supported by the Government.

But all the students do not get the help. The Government too has limitations like budget constraints. There is no coaching institution, which has a pan-India presence.

Of late, we have seen that interest in Civil Services is more in the students from rural areas. They score better then others in pass percentage. It is a welcome trend. We have also seen that the successful students coming from rural areas do well in their career too as soon as they join. Even then there are many aspirants who do not get proper coaching facilities. What I suggest is that some good coaching institutions should have an all-India presence. They should have their presence in capital cities, district headquarters and even in block headquarters. I think if they reach out nationally, a lots of things for guidance can be done for career development. It should not to be done as charity. They can do it as a business also, only the profit margin can be reduced. They can charge more from the students in urban areas and less from the students in rural areas. Because the income in rural areas is still meagre compare to the urban areas, the government can also subsidise such courses or coaching for the economically weaker sections of the society. All these efforts should be made to impart them quality training, timely guidance and also the basic necessities. They might have the knowledge, but they may not know how to express. That type of practical training at different levels is required.

Preparing for all Competitive Exams

If they conduct courses ranging from one month to six months duration, it can do well in enabling the rural students get into Civil Services and many other competitive examinations such as those for government or semi-government institutions, PSUs, banks, insurances, etc. Now many sectors are offering job opportunities. The coaching centres can prepare the students for those examinations and the rural students can do well too. So, the existing training or coaching institutions should increase their network giving more emphasis to the quality. It is not the number, which is important. Registering large numbers and collecting huge fees from them is not desirable. Whatever number they can handle should be taken. Overcrowding, making bigger classrooms and imparting training for namesake are not desirable. It's tantamount to exploiting the sentiments of the people.

Dignity of Labour

Another thing is that the students should also remember that not everyone will get into the Services. Only the bright students will get into. Then what will others do? It is competition. Everyone will not succeed because there are not so many opportunities. The other people who do not make it in first or second attempt, should not get disheartened. They should always have hope. Because life is sustained by hope. Whatever job they get, they should take that up. We all should have dignity of labour. No job is superior or inferior. We should be ready to do any kind of job for survival. Because survival is what is important. If you work hard and earn money for survival, nothing is bad. That is the value that all the students must imbibe. It is very important.

Sky is the Limit

Dignity of labour is required in India. It is for all of those who are preparing. They should have in mind that whatever job we get is good. No job is small or no job is big. Accept that job and then move on. Once you get into a job, you can always move on. There is no limit for the educated person. Rather sky is the limit. Those who have done tenth standard they can do subsequent studies through correspondence course. They can acquire degrees from open universities. They too can get into Services. Efforts should continue. That is what is important and required. So, I would say that hard work, dignity of labour and self-confidence are the key factors. If we make up our mind and make good efforts, nothing is impossible for a human being. We can achieve everything. All individuals have the capacity. Because the God has not discriminated. God has given us the same capacities. That we should understand.

□

Preparation Mantra for Civil Services

Many things are required by an individual while preparing of the Civil Services examinations conducted by the Union Public Service Commission (UPSC). First, the individual has to make his/her mind as what he/she wants to become. So, the goal has to be set. Having set the goal, the efforts have to be made to achieve that goal. If one sets the goal very high and does not make efforts accordingly, then it becomes a pipe dream.

No Short-Cut to Hard Work

There are people who, during preparations of Civil Services exams, even stop applying for other examinations, which is incorrect. We may have target of becoming civil servant, but we should apply for other exams too. Whatever chance they get that should be utilised properly. Once they get success in any examination, it increases the confidence. If they are financially self-sufficient they can continue to prepare for the next exam. That should be the strategy. Not that I want to become an IAS, and nothing else. That type of target setting may prove costly, if one does not get success. Because there are many factors that affect the Civil Services exams.

What works in real life is the hard work. There is no short cut to hard work. Passing the Civil Services exam does not happen in one or two years' time. It requires consistent efforts. A person has to prepare consistently. His/her mind should completely be open. Whatever knowledge comes, should be absorbed and assimilated. When you appear for the exam, everything—relevant or irrelevant one has learnt—becomes relevant there.

Changing Pattern of Exams

For some time, the Civil Services patterns are changing fast and question-setting is becoming interesting. So, time management is essential. It is 99% perspiration and 1% inspiration. That is how it works. One single person, incident, teacher or peer group can inspire you to become a Civil Servant, but that is only the starting point. You have to make efforts and struggle hard for preparations, which will count to be 99%.

Be Confident in Interview

The other thing, which happens in Civil Services, is that they don't want to judge your knowledge alone. After passing the written exam, many people prepare for the interview. But many people do not perform well in the interview. People mug up a few questions and answers and try to act smart. They answer irrelevantly. They know that they do not know the answer, they still try to answer, which is not correct. When you face the interview board, you should be confident. Your knowledge has already been judged in the written exam. In interview, they see your confidence level—how you conduct yourself, whether you are bluffing, whether you are forthright. They expect you to be forthright and confident. Self-confidence must be there. They may pose a situational problem. At that time, you should impartially say what you feel. Always try to be positive and not negative. They expect negative answers. Your individual opinion may be negative, but while telling them you should be positive. You have to see the brighter side of the things, not the negative ones. This is how many people commit mistakes during interview.

Think with Maturity

Civil Service is, of course, like a gambling. If you are intelligent, have done well academically, it is not necessary that you will pass the Civil Services. It does not happen so. Some people who have not done well in the school exams, they pass the exam in their first attempt itself. There are various such examples.

Civil Service being the premier Service, the UPSC has still maintained its standard. That is why it still remains the top choice for most of the students. Lakhs of people apply for it every year. It is a structured examination system and the UPSC is doing a good job. So, all the aspirants who are preparing for the Civil Services have to think with maturity and intelligence. They should have a good vision. They should not shy away from hard work. Basic knowledge, not the advanced, should be there. Basic terminology should be clear to everyone. Once it is clear and the glossary of different subjects is there, it helps one understand the things.

Regional Languages not Inferior

The UPSC has now changed the system. The regional languages have also been granted importance. Earlier, it used to be only in English medium. There is no question of having complex now. In whatever language the student expresses, is accepted. Even then the knowledge of English is very necessary. If you are not taking exams in English medium, you should still know English. Lots of content is available in English on internet or in the libraries, news, journals, etc. English has become a necessity. But, people should not develop any kind of complex. Those who know regional languages are also intelligent, more practical or pragmatic. That should not come in the way. What is most important is self-confidence. They should have full command and control over the subject. Any question is asked they should be thorough in that.

□

Competitive Exams: How to Crack the Nut

Different kinds of competitive exams are conducted throughout the year. The students, however, do all that they can to crack these exams, it is necessary to understand the basics to face such exams. These exams are basically designed to check the students' knowledge and its application in certain sections. Here are some techniques to prepare for a competitive exam—be it for IAS, IPS, IFS, KAS, SSC, IBPS, Insurance, NDA, etc. students should update their knowledge in versatile subjects like Current Affairs both National and International, Science, Medicine, Environment, Information Technology, Geography, History, Space, Education, Policy, Finance, Political Systems, Social Justice, Ethics, International Relations and so on. They should also be vigilant about the happenings across the globe. Students should also read newspapers, especially the editorial columns, listen to radio and watch news channels-both National and International. Specific goal, imagination, innovation, determination, positive thinking, persistence and hard work lead to success. Some keys to success are as follows:

Know the Things

There are certain things a student must know before he/she starts preparing for a competitive exam. Competition is always high in such exams and they must never give up hope and confidence. If a student starts something, it is not advisable to stop until unless he/she completes it. If one door closes, another one opens.

Know Your Exam

Before starting the study, a student must know everything about the exam for which he/she prepares. It is even more necessary if the student is applying for the first time. Collect some details of that exam and the concerned organisation also. Explore previous year's syllabus, details and other statics. Also, read the syllabus carefully and understand everything you must know.

Analyse Yourself

Once the student knows everything about the exam, analyse where you stand right now. A student can take the help of sample papers, previous years' question papers and mock tests. This analysis helps him/her to find out the things he/she is strong at and also the things he/she needs to study more. Make a list of the topics and subjects accordingly.

Plan Smartly

Once the student has made up his/her mind to prepare for a competitive exam or to enter a particular sector, the most important thing is to plan your way. Get a rough idea when these exams are conducted in a given year and calculate how much time you have for your preparation. In the entire competitive exam, what is essentially required is the student's presence of mind. Studying till the last moment will only lead to stress and exhaustion. Before formulating the preparation strategy, chalk out the syllabus and measure comfort level in each section. Suppose one feels that he/she is not good in reasoning or essay writing, divide the timetable accordingly and give extra time to the area where is the lacunae.

Make a List

Once the candidate has a sense of the syllabus, make a list of the books or study material required for the exam. Study material for the areas like Verbal Abilities, Math and English should be collected.

Break-up of Time

Make a daily timetable and do not forget to include recreational activities in it. Also, try to shuffle the subjects so that it does not get boring. One should try studying for at least four hours a day. Take time out for reading newspapers daily. 30 minutes would suffice for this; it will certainly help prepare for general awareness section.

Prepare Notes

Whatever the candidate studies, he/she must try to maintain a notebook for it. Go through this notebook while revising.

Set a Finishing Date

Set a finishing date on your mobile, calendar or put it on table. By this date, one should finish learning new concepts. It is important to stick to this date. After this, one can start applying what is learnt and see the performance by giving mock tests, practice previous years' papers, etc.

Quantitative Aptitude

Quantitative Aptitude should be given utmost importance at the time of preparation. Try practicing questions daily. Go through the concepts first and then solve problems. Make a note of important formulae, theories and corollaries. One should be thorough with tables, square roots and cube roots to do calculations quickly. Quantitative questions are not difficult to solve, all you need are practice and speed to excel in this section.

Enrich your Vocabulary

Improving vocabulary will help a great deal in the English section. Questions on Synonyms, Antonyms and One Word Substitution will become an easy nut to crack. This is the part which is not given due importance by majority of students. Having good vocabulary will do no harm. Instead it will help in Group Discussion and Interview Round (only if the student wishes to sweep others by command on the language using some flowery words).

Reasoning

Practice questions on age, direction and distance, seating arrangement and Venn diagrams as they are asked in almost every competitive exam. One should also work on one's speed. Try learning or making your own short cuts to solve a particular set of questions. This is the part where one cannot cram anything.

Along with all these techniques, commitment, hard work, sincerity, positive attitude, killer instinct and drive to achieve make one competent. If these steps are taken seriously while preparing for Civil Services, the success would not elude them for long. The key to success is embedded in all of us. We all have the potential to do anything we want. What we really need are the strong will, determination, hard work and positive attitude. Rest would happen automatically.

□

Role of Language in Administration

Breaking the Barriers by Learning Kannada after Cadre Allotment in 1986

After the completion of Foundation Course and beginning of the main training in administrative services, the cadre allotment takes place. Before that, nobody knows where one will be going. Everybody seems happy until the cadre allotment. Once the cadre is allotted, some are very happy as they get the state of their choice, while some are quite unhappy as they do not get either of their home state or the neighbouring state.

Cadre Allotment

The cadre allotment system at our time was very interesting. Before 1985 batch, there was a zonal system where one third of the selected people got their home states while two third were adjusted in neighbouring zones. So, most of the people used to land up in their neighbouring states. But the Government of India changed the cadre allotment system following extremism in Punjab. One third got their home states, while others were put on roster arranging the vacancies of states alphabetically. It was like lottery. Somebody got Andhra Pradesh, some Arunachal Pradesh, some Kerala or any other state.

I was allotted Karnataka cadre. When I came to know about my first posting in Lingasugur, I could not find where it is on the map of India, as it was very remote area. We thought of it as destiny. Initially, we also felt that it was like uprooting one from one's area and transplanting in some other area. You are basically uprooted from your entire cultural area, background, etc. My mother had not heard anything about Karnataka. When I informed her, she asked how far it is. Is it far away from Iran also? She knew about Iran because lots of people used to go there for work. Then, I informed her about it, that it is in our own country and it is beyond Bombay, as she had heard about Bombay, now Mumbai.

Learning Kannada

Immediately, after cadre allotment, one has to learn the language of that area. Language teachers are there in the Institute. So, I joined the classes and started learning small sentences of Kannada. Gradually, interest in the language developed. When we came as Probationers, we were allowed to engage a teacher and some allowance was paid for that. We had to pass tenth standard in Kannada. However, earlier, it was fourth standard.

After joining the duty, I deeply realised that knowing the language is a must as without learning the language you cannot identify yourself with the people. You cannot manage with English alone. In old days, people could get away with English because there was less contact with the public, but it is no longer possible now. If you do not speak Kannada, you are treated as an alien. The best way, I realised, to reach out to people and to understand them is to learn their language. Language is a gateway for an Administrator. If you talk in their language, they immediately identify with you. Otherwise the moment you don't speak their language, you become an outsider for them. Language in that way is a great barrier and a leveler too. If you speak the language of the people, you will be able to understand their grievances and respond to them.

Real Encounter with the Language

The actual learning of the language began when I was posted in the field. Everything came in Kannada, including Tapal, noting, etc. It was difficult to read the hand-written things. So, I used to call my officials and even the PA to read what was coming in the Tapal. And they read out orally. And then I would listen what is written there. Many a time very interesting words came, which I heard for the first time. The word 'lunch' in English is used for afternoon meals, but in Kannada it is used for 'bribe'. Similarly, in Hindi the word 'Uchita' is used for good thing, but in Kannada it is different. You may see the Sanskrit words, but their meanings have different connotations.

Right from the beginning, I did not have any reservation in learning a new language. I started speaking and making notes in Kannada. Now, I have internalised the language in such a way that for me it has become equivalent to my mother tongue. When I went to Rajasthan, and got a taxi, I instructed the driver in Kannada. The fellow did not react. Suddenly, I realised I am in Jaipur. And then immediately I switched over to Hindi. It happens many times. Sometimes when you speak Hindi, some Kannada words come to the tongue. In my village, when we are sitting with someone, suddenly Kannada words come out without any realisation. I have become very native to this place in my 30 years of service.

Translation Cannot Convey the Feelings

Actual learning of my Kannada was during my first posting in Raichur. Learning a language is like swimming. You may theoretically know how to swim. But you learn swimming only when you are practically in the water. Similarly, you can get a lecture on riding a bicycle, but actual driving is learnt when you start paddling it. Language learning is a skill. It is a must today. You see the businessmen; they learn different languages only to communicate effectively with their customers. In administration, language is the key to success. Without overcoming language barriers one cannot become a good administrator. After all, you are there to solve their problems. Translation cannot convey the feelings. To connect with them knowing the language is a must.

Somebody has rightly said that one language sets you in a corridor for life. Two languages open every door along the way. If you talk to a man in a language he understands, that goes to his head. If you talk to him in his language, that goes to his heart.

□

I did what I Thought was Right

Wherever I worked during my Service period, I firmly did what I thought was right. If it was possible to decide the matter, I decided without wasting the time, and if it was not possible or not required or I felt was not appropriate, I did not do that even after repeated pressures. I worked in different capacities, but everywhere I followed this principle. That is why I left my imprints in almost every Department, even if I worked there only for a few days.

Total Revamp of Land Army Corporation

After coming back from the Government of India, I was posted in the Land Army Corporation for three months. In those three months alone, we formulated plans, motivated the staff and revamped the Department to the extent that it successfully competed with the private players in the field of construction. We had even decided to share the profit with the staff, which is normally not done in the government sector. Thereafter, I was shifted to the Housing Board.

'100 Housing' Scheme in BDA

When I went to the Housing Board, it was not in a good financial condition. However, the condition of Housing Boards in other states too was not good. The major problem in Karnataka was that the image of the Housing Board had deteriorated badly in public. So, the immediate task before us was to restore the image. We knew that the image would not improve without doing anything concrete. The Board had lot of land in different parts of the state. We identified 100 locations and conceived '100 Housing' scheme at those locations. We put the project on a fast track basis like the private builders do. We called for competitive bids, empanelled architecture firms and tendered out to agencies on Turnkey basis. There was no acceleration clause. Once the tender was awarded, it was the responsibility of the bidder to complete the project in that amount and timc limit only.

The idea clicked and it generated huge demand for the houses built by the Housing Board. However, initially, people were skeptical about the quality of houses, but when they personally saw third party inspection and high quality material being used, lots of people applied for the houses. There was tremendous demand in Mandya, Mysore and Bidar. Since land cost was not much, the housing units were very reasonable. I was there only for two years and in that duration we brought most of the houses to completion. We allotted most of the houses to the people and there still was a huge demand from different locations.

Unprecedented Reforms in BESCOM and KPTCL

We were in the process of taking up joint development activities in the Housing Board, but then I was shifted to BESCOM, where too several reforms were initiated including administrative reforms, training, motivating to staff, computerisation of billing system, 24×7 payment kiosks, online energy audit, etc. Massive SCADA work was also taken up. All the 66 KV and above capacity stations were operated remotely. In similar ways, we used technology in KPTCL too.

Refurbishing Social Welfare Department

From KPTCL, I was posted to Social Welfare Department as Secretary. The Department had huge resources and network of institutions, but all were poorly managed. The condition of SC/ST hostels was very poor. The quality of teachers was poor, motivation level low and making of false bills was taking place on a large scale. We tried to streamline the entire system. For the first time in 2006, we introduced biometric attendance for the students in hostels. Thus, bogus billing was curbed substantially. At that time the tendering used to be done at the District level. We empowered the hostel superintendents and their seniors to buy certain items such as milk, vegetables, etc. locally. Then we imparted training to 14,000 staffers including hostel wardens, supervisors, cooks and others. Using the satellite network of SIRD, the then Minister of Social Welfare and I addressed the staff of all 170 taluks. We exposed them to training. Such large scale training was never done in one single day. We did it sitting in Mysore through satellite only. The staff was also surprised and many of them said they were never exposed to such training in their entire period of service. Then we brought about a compendium for the hostels, which included dos and don'ts. All that was put in a booklet. Likewise, we tried to bring lots of reforms in Karnataka Residential Educational Institutions Society (KREIS) or Morarji Desai Schools run for SC/ST and OBC students in rural areas. However, all that was not unopposed. Anything you plan to do, there is always a counter view. If you are able to tackle the hurdles, you can bring about the change. That is what I have experienced. In fact, we had planned lots of ICTUs like content development, satellite training, extra classes, etc. What I have introduced in Higher Education Department in 2016 had been planned for those hostels at that time.

Making Bangalore the Most Beautiful Metro City

After Social Welfare Department, I was shifted to BBMP in 2009. Since there was no elected body in BBMP then, it was a big challenge. The expectations of the Government and the people were high. You have to face a new problem every day in the city. Apart from looking after the daily affairs, I planned 800 km four-lane road in the city. We had fixed the agencies and tender was almost concluded. But then some people went to the court and we had to stop that. We had taken up road widening in a big way and around 25% work was done.

We had also planned segregation at source programme to dispose of the waste. At that time, we took over most of the lakes from Lake Development Authority. We surveyed all the lakes and listed 186 lakes. Encroachments were identified and action was taken to remove the encroachments. Then we started fencing the lakes. Whatever fencing and stone pillars you see today were erected then only. It stopped further encroachment. We also took up fascinating paintings on the walls of the city. We assigned some themes to the local painters who did that on large scale. It generated awareness about the tourist places and Kannada heritage. It was a big hit.

One Citizen, One Tree

After BBMP, I was shifted to BDA where too we took up lots of plans. One of the major projects was making the Ring Road signal-free by building 15 flyovers. We also solved the Arkavathy problem, which had hugely dented the image of the BDA. We had planned to expand the Ring Road, as almost half of the city does not have Ring Road. Many flyovers were left out. We wanted East, West, North, South elevated corridor. Wherever Metro Rail is crossing today, we had planned road there by using the same pillars. Metro could have gone one stage above the elevated corridor. In BDA, we had also planned to plant one crore saplings. We successfully planted about 35 lakh trees. But, subsequently that was not continued. Otherwise we could have easily reached the one crore figure. The idea was to have one tree for every citizen in Bangalore.

□

Understanding the Rural Woes

Born and brought up in a village of Rajasthan, the village life is very much familiar to me. After I joined the Lal Bahadur Shastri National Academy of Administration (LBSNAA) in Mussoorie, then too we were sent to different villages of various states so that we can see the village life closely and also understand the problems faced by the people there.

Dignity of Labour

As part of the village visit, we Probationers were sent to a village of Punjab. The Sarpanch had already been informed about the visit. One Sardarji was the Sarpanch of the Panchayat. We were housed in a school ensuring all the necessary facilities for us. The school had indeed been turned into a guest house. Since Punjab is a very prosperous state, the villages there too are very prosperous. Land is very fertile. Coming from Rajasthan, I could see the contrast between the two states. We studied all aspects of the Panchayat there—how farming is done, how people get labour from outside and how they themselves work in the farms. The dignity of labour was a good thing there. Every farmer himself worked in the field. Even if they held any high position, even an elected representative like an MLA, they, if in the village, took active part in the farming activities. It is a good thing, which is not found in many other parts of the country. Contrary to it, in Rajasthan lots of women work in the field and men work less. In Punjab, both men and women are hard workers.

Promoting Judicious Use of Water

When I was posted in Karnataka, the experience of my village life in Rajasthan and also the experience gained in Punjab helped me a lot to understand the contrast between the village life in Karnataka and in those states. The areas like Lingasugur were more akin to Rajasthan. Irrigation was very less and even drinking water problem was there. Of course, in some parts of Lingasugur, like in Sindhanur, we have irrigation through Tungbhadra. But, I found people were using excess water. There was wastage of water. In contrast, there was no water in Lingasugur. It was mainly dry and dependent upon rain. Another Taluka, Kushtigir, was also a dry area. The position there was still bad. Though a river passes through those areas, they were hardly irrigated. Narayanpur Dam was constructed. So, most of the water was stored there itself. Hardly was there any water in the river. I saw both the regions—wastage as well as shortage of water.

Contrary to it, there was no wastage of water in Punjab. They use water judiciously. Similarly, the awareness about farming was very less in some parts of Karnataka. The impact of Green Revolution too was very less compared to Punjab. This way we could see the village life here, in Rajasthan and in Punjab. We could compare these three places—how people live.

Innocent People

We also saw that people in rural areas of Karnataka are very innocent. They believe so much in the Administration. They are less aware of their rights and are less demanding. They are very obedient. One can see it clearly. It was more in Raichur, because in the old days of Nizams, it was part of Hyderabad and Karnataka Region. Lingasugur used to be the District headquarters in the olden days. Urdu was used as main language there. There has been high regard for the Administration, especially for the senior officers like the

Assistant Commissioner, Tehsildar, Revenue Officer and even the Police Officer, which is not there in Punjab, where people are more aware of their rights.

Keeping the Doors Always Open

The situation in Rajasthan is akin to Karnataka. We could compare and see how the villages are here and elsewhere. Good thing for me was my village experience of Rajasthan and Punjab. It helped me appreciating the problems of the villagers. Whenever, I see villagers coming from any part of the state, I am the first person to call and meet them. Because of that background, I decided not to have any official timing to meet people. I have followed this rule right from the beginning.

I believe that there is no point in fixing the meeting time for those people. Because people from far away places do not come considering your timings. It depends upon several things—like what time they get the bus to come and what time they get the bus to return, etc. Apart from meeting the officer, they also do many other things in the city. So, we can't fix a timing to meet those people. I always thought it as artificial. I never thought of fixing any official time for meeting the people.

I always kept my doors open. Whenever I am free, I meet people. I have cultivated that habit since the beginning. This helped me in resolving many problems of the villagers including the problems of electricity and other things too. I always preferred to solve any grievance of the public on the spot if it was possible. It is my practice since the beginning.

Village people are very hard working and if they decide upon something they do it. If you honestly take them into confidence, they are always ready to wholeheartedly join hands in any constructive activity. I have experienced it throughout my career as an Administrator in the state.

□

Balancing Personal and Official Duties

Maintaining a balance between personal and official life is a big challenge for the public servants. Whenever they mix both, they suffer acute distress. If there is healthy balance between both, the life becomes easier. During my long career as an Officer of Indian Administrative Service (IAS), I have tried to maintain a balance between my personal and official duties. One has to face some emotional turning points also in the individual life. How we behave at that moment becomes a precedent for others to follow. If we lose the balance, it turns out to be a laughable situation.

Father Unwell

I remember an incident. My father, who then lived in our ancestral village in Rajasthan, was unwell. He was asthmatic. I brought him to Bangalore from Rajasthan so that I can take good care of him and also my work should not suffer. Then the election process was going on, but father's health was also not well. Though the doctors were trying their best, the recovery was not satisfactory. So, he required constant attention. That is why I asked for exemption from election duty. But, the Election Commission did not permit exemption then. Therefore, I had to devote time to the election duty too. I had to take my father to hospital whenever the doctor advised.

My father was aware of the seriousness of my duty. One day he himself did not tell me to accompany him to the doctor, but he expected me to be with him. So, he told the boy working with us to 'ask Saheb whether he is coming to hospital today'. The boy told me. I said, yes I would come. So, in the morning first I went to the hospital with him and consulted the doctor. The doctor said everything was all right. Then I sent the father back home and I went to office. I was holding the meeting of officers of SCOMs. At around 5.00 pm, I got a call from my daughter from home. She asked me to come home urgently. I asked what the matter was. She said Grand Pa is serious.

Father No More

I abruptly closed the meeting and quickly left for home. I did not tell anyone anything in the office. On the way, I told the PRO to ring up to the doctor. They called the doctors, who had reached home before I reached. They examined the father. I also reached home by then. In the evening, the father was all right. He went to the toilet on his own and ate some fruits. He asked whether we had more fruits. He was hungry. After eating fruits, he sat on the bed. But then probably there was sudden heart attack and he collapsed there and then.

Since I had left office without informing anyone, people started enquiring. After reaching home, I informed the personal staff that my father is unwell. They came to know that he is no more much later. When I left office, I was completely disconnected and not emotional. Normally, my children never used to call, when I was in the office. I took the mortal remains of the father by flight to New Delhi and then from New Delhi to my ancestral village in Rajasthan to perform the last rites. I stayed in the village for some time to complete the formalities related to the last rites. Then I joined the office.

Though, I have a high-pressure job, I was managing both the home front and the office too. I have always tried to keep a healthy balance between the home and office. I never took office to home or home to the office. Both are different things. My wife and children never know what I do during the day and what pressures do I face. When I go home, I don't bother anyone about the office happenings. Only in emergency, the things are managed. That is what I learnt in the beginning and still maintain.

Don't Mix Both Office and Home

Even if there is a crisis, I never looked under pressure or stressed. Both things are different. Office is different and home is different. The family should not bother about what is happening in the office, and office people should not bother about what is happening at home. Normally, many of us commit the mistake of mixing both the office and the home. Swami Vivekananda used to say, "Each duty has its own place, and according to the circumstances in which we are placed, we must perform our duties." We should focus on the things that are important to us, and should not do the extraneous stuff. Discipline doesn't come too naturally to most of us.

□

Expedition in an Unknown Territory

As we have to face so many challenges in our life every day, it naturally requires lot of energy to face them. We get physical energy from the food that we eat, but we also require the cosmic or spiritual energy to stay mentally fit. I have been a sort of atheist since my childhood—not believing in any form of God. I do believe that there is a supernatural power that probably controls the whole creation. As we see in Nature itself, there is a force beyond description starting from the Sun God, Mother Earth or natural creations. All these are manifestations of the supernatural existence.

I remember an incident of my childhood. My father's elder brother asked someone to predict what I would become in my life when I grow up. That man predicted that I would either become a big officer or a saint. I still remember those words. I used to like sitting in the company of elders for exchanging knowledge particularly on philosophy and spirituality. I was always curious to know more on these topics. However, after joining the Service, there is no time to sit with the elders, the spiritual aspect has always been there in the back of my mind.

The Magic of Cosmic Energy

Since the last four-five years, I have been in touch with a person who seems to be a realised soul. He taught me several aspects of *'kriyas'*. I practice those *'kriyas'* to gain spiritual power or energy from the Source. I found that the energy that we get from cosmos or outside keeps us going and we never feel tired and exhausted. Any time you take a deep breath and you feel as fresh as you were in the morning. It is an inexhaustible part of life. All around us, we can see it. We are enveloped by energy around us. This understanding has helped me in my work also. The work is generally stressful especially for the public officials where public contact is there. Like the job of Commissioner BBMP, BDA, Housing Board, electricity board, electricity companies, etc. all were very stressful and quite demanding. But with spirituality, I could have adequate energy as and when I needed. Every day, I had that experience. I never felt energy loss to fight the stress or to overcome the situation.

Seeing Harmony in the Whole

Spiritual dimension is something, which is individual and not connected to any sect, thinking, religion, etc. It is something, which is within all of us. At times, everyone requires it. This aspect helped me in several ways in my personality. Also, I found there to be no contradiction between the duty and pursuing the spirituality. Normally, most people associate spirituality with discarding everything or leaving the worldly stuff. Rather, I see harmony in the whole. Even while doing your job also you can remain indifferent. That is what I have learnt. In any stressful situation, I don't get disturbed. I always remain balanced and grounded to reality. Any type of work that we do, especially in public, is highly demanding. People expect too much and expect immediate results. Sometimes people come to provoke us to put us on the defensive. You can learn the art of avoiding such situations.

Test of Patience

I remember an incident when I was Deputy

Commissioner in Mangalore. There was a huge agitation by fishermen and others against the MRPL which was polluting the sea water and the surroundings. There was complete bandh along the NH 17. People were demonstrating everywhere including outside our office. We were sitting inside. A delegation was coming from backside of the DC Office through a congested area. I came to know that somebody from amongst them threw stone at a religious place there. It was around 4.30 in the evening. There was also firing during the day at the National Highway injuring a few people. So, it was quite a tense situation. When I came to know about the stone throwing at the religious place, I immediately called the leaders of the protest and told them in clear terms to call off the agitation forthwith. I told the leaders to sit in the government vehicle and tell the people that the agitation has been called off; otherwise they would all be put behind the bars for inciting communal tension. They were perplexed and easily sat in the government vehicle and started announcing that the agitation had been called off. Had we not taken that step, the agitation would have taken an ugly turn. They tried to provoke us and test our patience.

Going Beyond Mind and Body

Spirituality is a journey in an unknown territory. You don't know where you are going. And there is no defined way also. Nobody can tell you where you are going and what is the way? Everybody has to discover his/her own way in the spiritual progress. That is what my spiritual friend told me. That is a fact. Spiritual progress is something where you evolve over a period. This one thing is clear in the whole concept. We are prisoners of our own deeds. When a child is born, he/she is the most pious thing. It is so innocent and humble. That is why we call it a manifestation of God itself. There is nothing bad in the child. When the same child starts understanding things and perceptions around him/her, they become *sanskars*. Hence, we acquire lots of *sanskars* in our life, which never leave us.

The spirituality helps us overcome the negative *sanskars*, the energy or the experiences, which are not relevant. Mind is like a monkey, which has a new thought every second. One tries to concentrate on something, but it goes to something else. If you practise spirituality properly, it helps you go beyond mind and body. You can progress on the spiritual journey only if you go beyond your body and mind. If your mind still disturbs you and you continue to think about bad and good, you can never gain spiritual power. It is individual journey for the truth or realisation. It helps in your duties too. It makes you *'santoshi'* or self-contented. Your demands are limited. Greed does not overtake you. Those are the virtues, which help you. They helped me also in the long run.

Feeling Contented

Of late, I found that the spiritual aspect is something wonderful and that comes with understanding. If we really become evolved, then we do not feel difference between who is mine, who is not; or who is good or bad, you go beyond all that. You will not amass wealth or do anything wrong. You always feel neutral, contented and happy. Many such people are there in India. But what we do in normal day-to-day mundane world are rituals and not the spiritual things. What we do in temples or puja at home are all rituals not the spirituality. We have not gone beyond the rituals. We have unfortunately reduced spirituality or religion into rituals. We have idols in the temples. There is nothing in those idols. It is simple stone only in that sense. If the God was there in the statues how come the invaders could loot us and destroy the temples and even break those statues and why did Gods not punish them? It is only our belief that the statue has some power. Without thinking about the statue also, you can imagine the God.

Going Beyond Boundaries

If you go beyond statues or beyond the boundaries of temples, then you can connect to the supernatural power. In fact, man subsequently evolved certain forms of God. It is man's interpretation of what is God. Today we see the Sun. It is pure manifestation of energy. It gives life to the creation on the planet. That is the manifestation of God itself. See a plant. Human beings cannot create a plant. No scientist can create a living cell. They can manipulate the cell but cannot create. Then who has put life in the cell? Our entire history has been put in that one cell only. We have evolved over a period of time with that cell only. If you imagine something, it means you are still stuck in the control of mind only. This is how the whole world is experiencing a turmoil today. People are being butchered in the name of religion all over the world. Human beings suppress the people in one form or the other. These are the man-made things. Spirituality is much beyond this.

□

Imbibing Eternal Source of Energy

An Indian Administrative Service (IAS) officer has to work round the clock. From the first assignment that one takes up after joining the Service, till the last assignment one finishes at the end of the Service, most of the tasks are high pressure jobs. In the beginning of their career, they have to do mostly public oriented jobs. At times, it is very taxing, because they always have some problems in hand to resolve. There are lots of demands not only from the public and public representatives, but also from the office and home. It is quite demanding everywhere, which I have closely seen in my career. Therefore, the person who has to handle different types of critical situations has to have abundant source of power within. Then only they can cope up with the work stress. Sometimes, the situation takes so critical turn that the person handing it almost collapses under pressure.

Yoga – the Source of Energy

I remember several similar demanding assignments in Bruhat Bangalore Mahanagara Palike (BBMP) Bangalore Development Authority (BDA), BESCOM and also as Deputy Commissioner. I found that apart from the spiritual part, practicing yoga and other physical activities such as *'Asanas'* proved to be big source of power to face those challenging situations. Yoga, as we commonly know, is a union of two things—individual being with the higher being. So, when we practise yoga, it is not merely the physical exercise. Many people ascribe it to be the physical *Asanas*. It is beyond that. *Asana* is only the posture of the body. But if you go beyond that you find it is something different. If you take your mind away from the body or mental consciousness, that is the yoga wherein the union of individual soul takes place with the super consciousness or the Ultimate Being. That is how people in Hindu culture say the God is everywhere; we are part of the God, I am also God, etc. So, in every cell we see the God, because that is a creation of the Nature. That connection has to be established and that is possible through yoga.

I have realised that yoga helps in contemplation, keeping the body in shape and getting more and more energy needed to fight the stress and distress levels. It helped me right from the beginning. Apart from sports, I practise yoga and *'kriyas'* for almost two hours daily. I have found it to be very useful as an individual. Yoga is your personal journey. It has nothing to do with your office or anything else. It takes care of your body requirements. As the body requires food and rest, it requires yoga also for energy. As you need good nutritious food to cultivate your body into shape, you also need to have your distress levels away from you. You should not take your anxieties with you. You should not sleep with your anxieties.

Relaxation through 'Yognidra'

All these things seem to be good to hear or share with others. But in practice, it does not happen, because we find it difficult to distinguish between home and office. Most people mix up home and office. Some people do not dissociate themselves with work. They emotionally get attached to the job. Whereas in bureaucracy, it is not supposed to be done. You are supposed to be impersonal, indifferent and not connected with the matter. One is however physically connected, one has to dispose of the files and take the views, but there is no personal stake in the whole decision making. That is how one has to make impartial decisions. That is expected in the system. But if you take the things personally, then you will get biased. If you don't get detached from the office or take the things personally, your stress levels will be high. That realisation does not come automatically. It comes with experience and practicing yoga among other things.

One of the good practices taught in most yoga institutions is *'yognidra'*. It is a process of taking awareness to various parts of the body. In this process you are aware and not sleeping. But you are transported to a different level—beyond your mind and body—and consciousness is concentrated in different parts of the body in a specified manner. Half an hour of *'yognidra'* gives you so much of relaxation that it is equal to two hours actual sleep. So, you get four times more energy through this method. That is the power of yoga.

Avoid Overdose

Yoga has to be done as per individual capacity. There is no text prescription for all these things. Whatever your body demands or whatever rest you require, can be achieved through this relaxation exercise, which can be done in any position sitting, lying, etc. One cannot insist to sit in Padmasana only. If somebody does not have legs, how can he/she sit in the Padmasana? Equally, if you insist to sit straight, if somebody has problem how can he/she sit in that position? But that does not mean that he cannot do relaxation exercises. Anyone can do it anywhere, and at any time. My experience is that do what your body is used to. One should not stretch the body beyond its capacity. Overdose is not good. Yoga is a tremendous source of energy, because energy is everywhere outside. But the body takes only what it requires. Yoga helps you to connect with the outside energy faster. Sports activities are not as good as yoga. I found it very useful personally.

Negativity always damages. Negative thoughts create negative energy only. Whereas positive thoughts create positive energy. It is all in the thought process. When a bad thought comes in the body, the whole body feels sad. You think of a bad event in your life, the whole body immediately goes silent. It brings a bad effect in the whole body. It affects every part of the body. It is not the mind that is affected by anything, it is the parts of the body, which are affected—emotions, heart and other such things. Yoga helps you to eliminate negativity and gives more scope for positive thoughts. You get the sense of discrimination also—to discriminate between what is good and what is bad; I am different; it is my life; it is one life only; I will not get multiple lives, etc. After all, nobody is sure whether he/she would get second life.

Tips for Rejuvenating the Body

Competitiveness also creates anxiety in you. It demands more energy and one has to work hard. When your energy level is down, do one simple thing—just have 10 deep breathes, the whole body will get rejuvenated. We are connected with the outside world through the breath only. It is a science, but is very simple. There is a mechanism inside the body to convert the energy. It is there in animals and plants too. We are connected twenty four hours. It is like a gas cylinder. The stove is connected to the gas. As long as gas is there, it will burn. The moment the gas level is down, nothing will burn. The body is also like that only. The gas connection in our body is outside and it is through the breath only. If you are angry, your breath is very slow. If your body's tension level is high, you take breathe quickly. If you take ten deep breaths, your anxiety and anger will go away and you will get rejuvenated. The solution is with us, but nobody tells about it. If somebody tells, we do not follow that. What creates stress is that you are not able to control your emotions and gradually the level of anxiety goes beyond limits. It lands you into depression. That is how the personality problems develop.

Significance of Individual Discipline

Apart from yoga, individual discipline is also very important in life. We should not eat junk food. We should try to take the diet, which is rich, simple, less cooked, not overcooked and closer to nature. There are millions of varieties of animals. The prime difference between the animals and the human beings is only the intelligence, nothing else. Then which animal cooks food? None. It is only the man, which cooks. The man has only devised various cuisines and tastes. After the food goes beyond your tongue, it is all the same—no taste inside. The foods, which are closer to the nature, provide more nutrition. Therefore, we should try to take more fruits and vegetables. There is more energy in the raw food. When you put it in a pressure cooker or overcook it, the essence goes away. You may feel that your stomach is full, but essence will not be there. So, along with yoga, your lifestyle, food habits, going to bed early and getting up early are also important.

Earlier, I used to take non-vegetarian food at times. Now, since the day I started practicing yoga I automatically do not feel the desire for that. I have given up eating eggs too. If you are spiritually warm and practice yoga in perfect form, you do not feel the need for it at all. It is the good way of life and we have to popularise it. But for some time, even the yoga has become like a cult—power yoga, my yoga, art of doing something, etc. People have named it differently, but the original product is one i.e. connecting with the higher being. It connects with the power within you. And there are various ways to connect it.

□

Purifying the Soul through Karma Yoga

We have a right to work, but we don't have a right to the results of our actions. This is Karma Yoga or the yoga of action. This approach can save us from a lot of misery and bring us closer to the God. I have realised it in my life. In fact, you don't even need to believe in God to practice this yoga.

What is Karma Yoga?

We can see Karma Yoga in everything. The love between a child and mother needs no explanation. Mother never expects anything from the child. So much is her dedication to the child that she can even sacrifice her life for the child without any hesitation. You just do your best and leave the rest to the Almighty. This is the Karma Yoga. The result is bound to happen. Generally, the Karma Yoga is associated with the good or bad deeds committed in previous birth. But the real concept of Karma Yoga teaches many things—don't involve in any work too much, indifference towards the work, not expecting results immediately, etc. However, it is very difficult for a common man to get detached from work, because we practically start the work only after deciding the goal and then make efforts to achieve that goal. But the Karma Yoga, explained in Gita, says that you continue doing the job expected from you in whatever position and do not expect results.

Sense of Dedication

We play many roles in life. During our childhood, we are sons and daughters of our parents. Then we are children for the neighbourhood and the relatives. Our role is that we have to respect and obey them. During study, we are expected to excel and not to cheat the parents. After study, we become part of the society as active members. After marriage, we play the roles of husband or wife. In office also, we are either a leader or a co-worker. Our role towards the office, work, family, relatives or society is different. Our roles vary from time to time and keep shifting. But one thing is certain. In various capacities as a human being if we have a sense of dedication, we enjoy the whole process of working for others not working for self.

The people normally have a bad impression about bureaucracy. They talk loosely because of their bad experience. Of course, there are instances of bad response from the Administration, but there are many others who do their job sincerely. Everybody is not bad or corrupt. There are good people too, but what they do is not highlighted. Being part of the bureaucracy, it is not our duty to think that we should take responsibility for everything or we should think that we can change everything. But at least within our sphere of influence we should definitely try to make difference. Things get affected by our actions and good results too come. People watch them.

Genuine Intention

In most of my postings I have tried to work closely with the people and public representatives and found that people in general are very intelligent. They quickly find out and assess your level of commitment—whether you are talking from the bottom of your heart or you are just influencing them through causal talk. If they come to know that you are genuine, your intensions are good, you really want to do something good for the society or you want to involve them genuinely, they come forward unconditionally. Not at one place, but at hundreds of places I have realised it. In most of the circumstances I have found that people are not wanting. They are much more forthcoming. They want to give whatever they have just to be with you. This is the great quality of people. The welfare schemes of the government have to be delivered though the official system only. The public is not expected to do that. But if you really want to involve them in that process, they come forward. Of course, there are some bad elements in the society and good people may not be in the forefront, but once you go to them, you find lot of genuine people coming together to join hands.

Indifference towards Results

Innumerable examples are there when people took up even bigger tasks than expected from them. A dam has been constructed in Bijapur District of Karnataka by people alone. They thought of constructing a barrage across the Krishna River and soon it became a movement. The involvement of people in white revolution or milk production is also well known. However, similar active involvement has not been witnessed in other fields of cooperatives. In Maharashtra, the cooperative system, especially in banking and growing cash crops, is very strong. It is interesting to read so many such incidents in our epics also.

When I took more to spirituality, I became more indifferent to results. However, since beginning I have never been influenced by anything unduly. I faced challenges boldly—both internal and external—without expecting results. Doing good work or bringing about some changes within the system is still more difficult. It is easy to work in a controlled environment or a company, because there you know who are the people involved, you can hire and fire them. But in government you have no choice. You have only the administrative control over the people who are working with you, you cannot throw them out when they are not working properly. You can do nothing if some bad apples are there in your team. You have to mend them and make them only work. That depends upon your leadership quality and motivation.

Plan Big for Bigger Results

One thing that I have ensured in my whole career is that I never asked anyone for a transfer in any particular department. I also never tried to bring people from other departments with me. Many people take 'them' together as their confidants. I have never done that. Rather, I tried to find the best among the available lot. When I went to KPTCL from BESCOM, I found so many systemic constraints were there. They were not able to supply power to even the paying category like the industry, etc because of overloading. When I went there, I asked the engineers as to how many sub stations they completed in a year? They said (it was around 2004-05) 'about 20 to 22 stations' in a year. When I studied the difference between the requirement and the system constraints, there was overloading everywhere and we were not able to add more stations. There was no redundant capacity of the station transformers. I just told the engineers in a casual manner that after one year I want to commission at least one new station every day i.e. 365 stations in a year. Their immediate response was "how is it possible? How can we jump from 20 to 365??" I told them to plan accordingly to make it possible. If we have to create 365 stations in a year, then we have to plan at least 700 stations. If you plan less, you will achieve less.

The one point agenda that I put forth was that people nowhere in Karnataka should suffer from system failure. The engineers asked for budget that I ensured. I motivated them with all kinds of support. We had then planned over 400 stations. Then I analysed why the Department commissions less number of stations. We found that different works of the station were done by different people. If one work was ready, another was pending due to somebody else. Station was being created by somebody, while lines were laid by somebody else. If lines were ready, the station was not ready. If station was ready, the lines were not ready. At some places, everything was ready, but transformers were not there. After discussion, we decided to club both the works—station creation and line work. Since the contractors were not getting transformers individually from the supplier in time, we collected the requirements of all the transformers and floated a separate tender. We ensured that when the station is ready we would provide the transformers quickly. We also curbed other difficulties like payment, etc. With active monitoring and pursuance, we, through the same engineers who in the beginning said it was impossible, commissioned more than 250 stations in one year. Rest of the planned stations came up next year. That means when you plan something, visualise and pursue it, you get the results. We did not involve outside agencies, but used the same staff and got the results. This sort of motivation has to be there. Those who do good work have to be encouraged and those who do not work have to be taken to task. There is no need to condemn anybody.

Constructive Use of Bad Fellows

Another thing that I have seen is that nobody is 100% good or bad. Bad fellows also have some good qualities. They may be good in PR or expression. We should use them as the spokesperson. We can use them to convince the people. You have to assess the good qualities of a bad person also. Those who are good for nothing, just isolate them so that they do not at least damage the reputation of the organisation. This way things can be done.

I remember an example of BESCOM. Until my posting there, the Department was issuing hand written electricity bills. They used to maintain ledgers. The meter readers took the reading, went back to office, submitted the reading, then the office generated the bills and then the bills were issued to the consumers. Obviously, there were lots of mistakes. That is why thousands of people queued up to the offices with complaints regarding their bills. As a lasting solution, we decided to computerise the whole system. When the process began, the employees' association started opposing it. They insisted they would write ledgers because they got some remuneration for that. I assured them that their remuneration would not be discontinued. But parallely we continued the process of computerisation. Within six months we bought computers, softwares, and even started providing hand held devices to the meter readers. With this, consumers started getting electronic bills on the spot. This reduced the percentage of errors substantially.

Loss Turns into Profit

Once we computerised the system, we found that the loss in the city alone was 15-20%. It was too much. Internationally, it was then 5-6% only. We started thinking over it again. We first decided to focus on the meter readers only. We found that during meter reading they cover one side of the street one day and the next side on the next day. There was no relation between the transmission network and their meter reading. There was also no connection between how the power was flowing and how the bills were generated. We decided to realign the whole process. The power is measured at the station and the distribution transformers. We put the meter reading schedule on paper according to the network by clubbing the number of consumers and distribution transformers. We told the meter readers to record the reading of one transformer area on single day itself. We also put meters on the transformers. By doing this we could know how much electricity was supplied by the distribution transformer and how much was billed. This way we could map all 12,000 transformers in Bangalore and also check the loss occurred. At some places it was around 40 to 50%. We then decided to check every meter in the areas where the loss was above 20% to check whether there was a fault in the meter or the meter was bypassed. In three months time, we set the system right. We then continuously monitored all the high loss making areas. Of course, there were mischiefs at meter reader level too. But the computerisation curbed power theft considerably. The complaints reduced substantially. It increased BESCOM's income up to ₹ 500 crore annually. This shows that we have to strengthen the system where it is weak.

Help, Heal and Share

Sometimes there are different kinds of challenges. During my posting in Electricity Department, we had to revise the salaries of the staff, as there was a wage revision after every four years. The Minister, who was also Chairman of the Electricity Board, got 12% hike approved from the Chief Minister. When we tried to implement the proposal in the Board, the same Minister refused to approve 12% hike and insisted on 10% only. Finally, we deferred the matter and kept it pending for some time. But the employees kept on pressurising us for it. Then I drafted the orders and sent the file to the Chairman. One day, he called me and said 'you want to be good with the employees'. I said, I do not need their votes. I have no interest. Either you change your order or implement it fully. Finally, he issued orders for implementation of the wage revision. Sometime, there is conflict between the policy and the practice.

Karma performed by right means does not harm anybody. This is Karma Yoga. To drop the doer from the action is Karma Yoga. To see oneself as a mere tool of the Divine and to offer the fruit of our actions to the Divine is the Karma Yoga. Karma Yoga means to help, heal and share.

□□□